Synge: A Celebration

Druid Synge: *Níl sí ag Éisteacht*

J.M Synge is the subject of this Romanticized oil study by Irish artist Seán Keating PPRHA. The dark woman is reputed to be a member of a family from the Aran Islands; however, if comparison is made with contemporary photographs it seems apparent that the image may also represent a Romanticized portrait of Molly Allgood to whom Synge was to be married before he died in 1909.

In *Níl sí ag Éisteacht*, a painting of great dramatic intensity, Keating has paid textured homage to Synge, the Irish Theatre, and the Aran Islands, all of which were of vital inspiration to his imagination and artistic career.

The painting is reproduced by kind permission of Sir and Lady A.J. O'Reilly. Copyright permission granted by the Keating Estate.

Éimear O'Connor

Synge: A Celebration

Edited by Colm Tóibín

Carysfort Press

A Carysfort Press Book

Synge: A Celebration

Edited by Colm Tóibín

First published in Ireland in 2005 as a paperback original by Carysfort Press, 58 Woodfield, Scholarstown Road, Dublin 16, Ireland. Reprinted August 2005

© 2005 Copyright remains with the authors

Typeset by Carysfort Press
Cover design by Alan Bennis
Printed and bound by eprint Limited
35 Coolmine Industrial Estate, Blanchardstown,
Dublin 15, Ireland

The publication of this work was supported by a Title by Title Award from the Arts Council.

Contents

Frontispiece   iv

Acknowledgements   ix

The Authors   xi

List of Illustrations   xvii

1 | New Ways to Kill Your Mother   1
Colm Tóibín

2 | A Gallous Story and a Dirty Deed: Druid's Synge   33
Fintan O'Toole

3 | Shift   47
Hugo Hamilton

4 | *A Glass of Champagne*   57
Marina Carr

5 | A White Horse on the Street   69
Vincent Woods

6 | Driving Mrs Synge   83
Sebastian Barry

7 | *Riders to the Sea*   91
Mary O'Malley

8 | Apart from Anthropology   101
Anthony Cronin

9 | Bad at History   115
Anne Enright

10 | Collaborators   125
Joseph O'Connor

11 | Wild and Perfect: Teaching
The Playboy of the Western World   139
Roddy Doyle

A PLAY IN ONE ACT

When the Moon Has Set   147
J.M. Synge
Introduction by Ann Saddlemyer

Acknowledgements

Special thanks, at the beginning, to Lilian Chambers and Dan Farrelly from Carysfort Press for their kindness and patience and careful hard work; also, to Rupert Murray, Fergal McGrath and Thomas Conway from Druid for the above in equal measure; then to Michael Stack, who worked as editorial assistant, for his patience and diligence; also, to the Trinity College Library and the staff of the Manuscripts Department. We are also indebted to Éimear O'Connor for her generous endeavours in acquiring permissions to use Sean Keating's painting for the frontispiece; and finally, to a number of scholars who have written on the life and work of Synge, and whose books and essays have been invaluable to us in the making of this collection, especially Ann Saddlemyer, Andrew Carpenter, W.J. McCormack, Declan Kiberd, Nicholas Grene and Roy Foster.

Authors

Sebastian Barry was born in Dublin and educated at Trinity College Dublin. He has been Writer Fellow, Trinity College Dublin, during 1995-1996, and has won numerous awards. His novels include *Macker's Garden* (1982), *Time Out of Mind* (1983), *The Engine of Owl-light* (1987), *The Whereabouts of Eneas McNulty* (1998), *Annie Dunne* (2002), *A Long Long Way* (2005). His plays include *Prayers of Sherkin* (1991), *The Only True History of Lizzie Finn* (1995), *The Steward of Christendom* (1995), *Our Lady of Sligo* (1998) and *Hinterland* (2002). He lives in Wicklow and is a member of Aosdána.

Marina Carr grew up in Co. Offaly. Her main theatrical works include *Low in the Dark* (1989), *The Deer's Surrender* (1990), *This Love Thing* (1991), *Ullaloo* (1991), *The Mai* (1994), *Portia Coughlan* (1996), *On Raftery's Hill* (1996), and *Ariel* (2002). Her awards include The Irish Times Best New Play Award, the Dublin Theatre Festival Best New Play Award in 1994 for *The Mai*, a McCauley Fellowship, a Hennessy Award, the Susan Smyth Blackburn Prize, and an E.M. Forster prize from the American academy of Arts and Letters. She is a member of Aosdána and lives in Kerry.

Anthony Cronin is a poet, novelist, memoirest, biographer, and cultural critic. His many works include the novels *The Life of Riley*, and *Identity Papers*. His collections of poetry include

Poems (1958), *Collected Poems, 1950-73* (1973), *New and Selected Poems* (1982), *The End of the Modern World* (1989); *Relationships* (1992), and *Minotaur* (1999). His non-fiction includes *Dead as Doornails* (1976), *Heritage Now* (1982/1983), and *Samuel Beckett: The Last Modernist* (1996). A play, *The Shame of it*, was produced in the Peacock Theatre in 1974. He has been associate editor of *The Bell* and Literary Editor of *Time and Tide*. In 1983 he received The Martin Toonder Award for his contribution to Irish Literature. He is a founding member of Aosdána, and lives in Dublin.

Roddy Doyle was born in Dublin and worked as a teacher before becoming a full-time writer in 1993. His novels are *The Commitments* (1987), *The Snapper* (1990), *The Van* (1991), which was shortlisted for the Booker Prize; *Paddy Clarke Ha Ha Ha* (1993), which won the 1993 Booker prize; *The Woman Who Walked into Doors* (1996), *A Star Called Henry* (1999), and *Oh, Play That Thing* (2004). His drama includes *War* (1989) and *Brownbread* (1993), as well as *The Family*, written for television. He has written the scripts for films based on his novels, including *The Commitments*, *The Snapper*, and *The Van*. He lives in Dublin.

Anne Enright was born in Dublin and is a novelist and short-story writer. She has published a collection of stories, *The Portable Virgin* (1991) which won the Rooney Prize that year. Novels include *The Wig My Father Wore* (1995), which was shortlisted for the Irish Times/ Aer Lingus Irish Literature Prize; *What Are You Like?* (2000), which won the Royal Society of Authors Encore Prize; and *The Pleasure of Eliza Lynch* (2002). Her stories have appeared in *The New Yorker*, *The Paris Review* and *Granta*. She was the inaugural winner of The Davy Byrne Award for her short story *Honey*. Her most recent work is a book of essays about motherhood, *Making Babies* (2004).

Hugo Hamilton was born in Dublin of Irish-German parentage. He has brought elements of his dual identity to his novels. *Surrogate City* (1990); *The Last Shot* (1991); and *The Love*

Test (1995). His short stories were collected as *Dublin Where the Palm Trees Grow* (1996). His later novels are *Headbanger* (1996); and *Sad Bastard* (1998). He has also published a memoir of his Irish-German childhood, *The Speckled People* (2003). In 1992 he was awarded the Rooney Prize for Irish Literature. He lives in Dublin and is a member of Aosdána.

Joseph O'Connor was born in Dublin. His first novel, *Cowboys and Indians* (1991) was shortlisted for the Whitbread Prize. This was followed by a volume of short stories, *True Believers* (1991) and four novels: *Desperadoes* (1993), *The Salesman* (1998), *Inishowen* (2000), and *Star of the Sea* (2002), which became an international bestseller and was published in 29 languages. It received the Prix Littéraire Zepter for European novel of the year, a Hennessy/Sunday Tribune Honorary Award, the Irish Post Award for Fiction, France's Prix Millepages, Italy's Premio Acerbi, a Nielsen-BookScan Golden Book Award, and an American Library Association Notable Book Award. His non-fiction includes *Even the Olives are Bleeding: The Life and Times of Charles Donnelly* (1993); *The Secret World of the Irish Male* (1994); *The Irish Male at Home and Abroad* (1996); and *Sweet Liberty: Travels in Irish America* (1996). He has written three stage plays: *Red Roses and Petrol* (1995); *The Weeping of Angels* (1997); and *True Believers* (2000). His screenplays include *A Stone of the Heart; The Long Way Home;* and *Ailsa.* He has recently been awarded a Cullman Writing Fellowship at the New York Public Library.

Mary O'Malley was born in Connemara, Co. Galway and educated at University College Galway. She taught for eight years at the University of Lisbon before returning to Ireland in 1982. Her collections of poems are: *A Consideration of Silk* (1990), *Where the Rocks Float* (1993); *The Knife in the Wave* (1997), *Asylum Road* (2001), and *The Boning Hall* (2002). She received a Hennessy award in 1990. Her next collection is due from Carcanet in 2006. She is a member of Aosdána, and lives in Connemara.

Fintan O'Toole was born in Dublin. He has been a columnist with *The Irish Times* since 1988 and was drama critic of the *Daily News* in New York from 1997 until 2001. His books include *The Politics of Magic: The Work and Times of Tom Murphy* (1987); *Ex-Isle of Erin* (1997); *A Traitor's Kiss: The Life of Richard Brinsley Sheridan* (1998); *Shakespeare is Hard But So Is Life* (2002); *After the Ball: Ireland After the Boom* (2003); and *White Savage: William Johnson and the Invention of America* (2005).

Ann Saddlemyer is Professor Emeritus of the University of Toronto and former Master of Massey College, currently adjunct Professor at the University of Victoria. She has edited the letters and plays of J.M.Synge, the plays of Lady Gregory, and the letters of the Abbey Theatre directors. She is one of the general editors of the Cornell Yeats manuscript project, and is currently working on an edition of the correspondence between George Yeats and W.B. Yeats. Her most recent book is *Becoming George: The Life of Mrs W. B. Yeats* (2003) which was shortlisted for the James Tait Black award.

Colm Tóibín was born in Enniscorthy, Co. Wexford and is a novelist and journalist. His novels are *The South* (1990), *The Heather Blazing* (1992/1993), *The Story of the Night* (1997), *The Blackwater Lightship* (1999), for which he was shortlisted for The Booker Prize, 1999; and *The Master* (2004). His non-fiction includes *Bad Blood* (1994) and *The Sign of the Cross – Travels in Catholic Europe* (1994). He recently won the Los Angeles Times Novel of the Year for *The Master*, which was also shortlisted for the 2005 Booker Prize. He lives in Dublin and is a member of Aosdána.

Vincent Woods is a poet and playwright. He was born in Co. Leitrim and has lived in the United States, New Zealand and Australia. He worked as a journalist with RTE until 1989, when he began writing full-time. His radio play, *The Leitrim Hotel*, was a prize-winner in the P.J. O'Connor Awards for radio drama and his poetry collections include *The Colour of Language*. His plays include *At the Black Pig's Dyke* (1992), *John Hughdy and Tom*

John (1991), *Song of the Yellow Bittern* (1994), and *A Cry from Heaven* (2005). Among his adaptations and translations are *Fontamara* (1998) and *Winter* (2005). He has won the M.J. McManus Award for Poetry and is a member of Aosdána

Illustrations

Cover   Watching the currach on its way to collect turf from a Galway Hooker. Synge photo 44 [TCD].

Frontispiece   J.M. Synge and Molly Allgood. *Níl sí ag Eisteacht* by Sean Keating PPRHA. Reproduced by kind permission of Sir and Lady A.J. O'Reilly. Copyright permission granted by the Keating Estate.

1   The Synge Family. [p.xviii]

2   Marie Mullen. [p.32]

3   Islanders on Inishere. [p.46]

4   J.M. Synge. [p.56]

5   Hotel Corneille, Paris. [p.68]

6   A Wicklow Tramp. [p.82]

7   *Riders to the Sea.*. [p.90]

8   Synge with his mother, Rosie Calthrop, and Annie Harmar. [p.100]

9   'Selling on the Stones'. p.114]

10   Molly Allgood. [p.124]

11   Aaron Monaghan. [p.138]

All photographs, except 2 & 11, are reproduced by kind permission of the Board of Trinity College.

Illustration 1: The Synge Family. (Seated, from left) Samuel, Mrs. Synge, John; (standing) Annie (later Mrs. Harry Stephens), Robert, Edward. TCD MS 6198/8

1 | New Ways To Kill Your Mother
Colm Tóibín

In 1980, having been evicted from a flat in Hatch Street in the centre of Dublin, I was offered temporary accommodation around the corner at Number Two Harcourt Terrace. The house, three storeys over basement, was empty, having recently been vacated by its elderly inhabitant. It was early April when I moved in and the cherry tree in the long back garden was in full blossom. Looking at it from the tall back windows of the house, or going down to sit in the garden under its shade, was a great pleasure. The thought might have occurred to me that whoever had just sold this house could be missing it now, but I don't think I entertained the thought for very long.

The aura of the previous inhabitant of this house, in which I ended up living for almost eight years and where I wrote most of my first two books, appeared to me sharply only once. I was putting books in the old custom-made bookshelves in the house when I noticed a book hidden in a space at the end of a shelf where it could not be easily seen. It was a hardback, a first edition of Louis MacNeice's 'Springboard: Poems 1941-1944'. I realized that these shelves must have, until recently, been filled with such volumes, and that the woman who had left this house and had gone, I discovered, to a nursing home, must have witnessed a lifetime's books being packed away, the books that she and her husband had collected and read and treasured. Books bought perhaps the week they came out. All lost to her now, including this one, which gave me a sense of her as nothing else did.

I asked about her. Her name was Lilo Stephens. She was the widow of Edward Stephens, the nephew of J.M. Synge. In 1971 she had arranged and introduced 'My Wallet of Photographs', by J.M. Synge. Edward Stephens, her husband, who died in 1955, was the son of Synge's sister Annie. Born in 1888, when Synge was seventeen, he was aged twenty when his uncle died in 1909. Later, he became an important public servant and a distinguished lawyer. In 1921 he accompanied Michael Collins to London for the negotiations which led to the Treaty. He was subsequently secretary to the committee which drew up the Irish constitution and thereafter became assistant registrar to the Supreme Court, and finally registrar to the Court of Criminal Appeal.

In 1939 on the death of his uncle Edward Synge, who had not allowed scholars access to Synge's private papers, Edward Stephens became custodian of all Synge's manuscripts. He began working on a biography of his uncle, which would partly be a biography of his family. 'I see J.M. and his work as belonging much more to the family environment,' he wrote, 'than to the environment of the theatre.' He had been close to his uncle, having been brought up in the house next door to him and spent long summer holidays in his company, and been taught the Bible by Synge's mother, as Synge had. But, in Synge's lifetime, not one member of his family had seen any of his work for the theatre. At his uncle's funeral, Edward Stephens would have had no reason to recognize any of the mourners who came from that side of his uncle's life. For his family, Synge belonged fundamentally to them; he was, first and foremost, a native of the Synge family.

'It was [Synge's] ambition,' he wrote,

> to use the whole of his personal life in his dramatic work. He ultimately achieved this ... by dramatizing himself, disguised as the central character or, in different capacities, as several of leading characters, in some story from country lore or heroic tradition. It is in this sense that his dramatic work was

autobiographical and that the outwardly dull story of his life became transmuted into the gold of literature.

In his work, Edward Stephens 'transcribed in full,' according to Andrew Carpenter

> many family papers dating back to the eighteenth century; he copied any letters, notes, reviews, articles, fragments of plays, or other documentary evidence connected, even remotely, with Synge. He also recounted, with a precision which is truly astonishing, the events of Synge's life: the weather on particular days, the details of views Synge saw on his bicycle rides or walks and the history of the countryside through which he passed, the backgrounds of every person Synge met during family holidays, the food eaten, the decoration of the houses in which Synge lived, the books he read, his daily habits, his conversations, his coughs and colds – and those of other members of the family.

By 1950, the typescript was in fourteen volumes, containing a quarter of a million words. On Stephens's death in 1955, it had still not been edited for publication.

His widow, Lilo Stephens, inherited the problem of the Synge estate. Out of her husband's work – 'the hillside,' as one reader put it, 'from which must be quarried out the authoritative life of Synge' – two books came. Lilo Stephens made her husband's manuscript available to David Greene, who published his biography in 1959, naming Edward Stephens as co-author. Later, in 1973, Andrew Carpenter would thank her 'for her patience, enthusiasm and hospitality' when he edited her husband's work to a book of just over two hundred pages, *My Uncle John*. In 1955, Lilo Stephens also had inherited Synge's papers from her husband. They had been kept for years in Number Two Harcourt Terrace as her husband worked on them. In 1971, Ann Saddlemyer would thank Lilo Stephens for first suggesting the volume 'Letters to Molly' and providing 'the bulk of the letters as well as much background material.' Edward Stephens had purchased these letters from Molly Allgood so that they would be safe. Finally, Lilo Stephens ensured the safety of Synge's entire archive by moving it from Harcourt Terrace to Trinity College where it rests.

Synge's family remains of great interest, either because of the apparent lack of any influence which they had on his work, or because they may or may not hold a key to his unyielding and mysterious genius. He seemed in his concerns and beliefs to have nothing in common with them – he stated that he never met a man or a woman who shared his opinions until he was twenty-three - and yet, for a great deal of his adult life, he lived with them and depended on them. Any version of his life and work has to take his family into account and understand the sense, in Edward Stephens' words

> that the context of his life … was quite different from any other writer of the literary movement. I tried to create a picture of a class or group in Irish society that has almost vanished.

If a writer were in the business of murdering his family, then the Synges, with their sense of an exalted and lost heritage and a strict adherence to religious doctrine added to a very great dullness, would have been a godsend. Synge's great-grandfather, Nicholas Grene tells us

> owned not only Glanmore [in County Wicklow], with its fifteen hundred acres of demesne including the Devil's Glen, but Roundwood Park as well, an estate of over four thousand acres.

His grandfather, however, managed to lose most of this property, a portion only of which was bought back by his uncle. Synge's father, who became a barrister, died when Synge was one year old. He left a widow, four sons, a daughter and four hundred pounds a year. The first three sons were solid citizens, becoming a land agent, an engineer and a medical missionary to China. The daughter married a solicitor. The youngest, it was presumed, despite his solitary nature and regular illnesses, would find eventually a profession to suit his family, if not his temperament.

In his book *Letters to my Daughter*, written in 1932, Synge's brother Samuel, the missionary, wrote:

> There is little use in trying to say what if our father had lived might have happened different to what did happen. But I think two things are fairly clear. One is that as your Uncle John grew up and met questions that he did not know how to answer, a father's word of advice and instruction would have made a very great difference to him. The other thing is that probably our father would have arranged something for your Uncle John to do besides his favourite reading, something that would not have been too much for him but would have brought in some remuneration at an earlier date than his writings did.

This was to consign Synge's mother Kathleen to dust, to suggest a sort of powerlessness for her. She was, in fact, a very powerful person. Synge's mother was born Kathleen Traill in 1838. Her father was a clergyman of whom Edward Stephens wrote:

> He spent his life, as he put it, waging war against popery in its thousand forms of wickedness, which did not always endear him to his ecclesiastical superiors.

Finally he became rector of Schull in County Cork where he died in 1847 from a fever caught from the people among whom he worked. His widow, who had been brought up in Drumboe Castle in County Donegal, moved to the southern suburbs of Dublin. From here in 1856, her daughter married John Hatch Synge, the playwright's father. They lived in Hatch Street in the centre of Dublin in the early years of their marriage, later moving to Rathfarnam where John Millington Synge was born. Later, after her husband's death, Kathleen Synge moved her family to Orwell Park in Rathgar.

Synge's paternal grandfather and his uncle Francis, who had bought back some of the family estates in County Wicklow, were members of the Plymouth Brethren. Mrs Synge's father had held strong evangelical views, which his daughter also shared. She brought up her children according to strict religious principles, and her social life, such as it was, seemed to include only people who were of a like mind and background. Edward Stephens wrote:

> Mrs Synge conducted her household by a rule as strict as that of a religious order and supposed that her children would acquiesce without question. She was very well versed in the doctrine to which she adhered and she could support every tenet by citing scriptural authority. She believed the whole Bible to be inspired and its meaning to be clear to anyone who read with an open mind and faith in the Holy Ghost.

In an autobiographical essay written in his mid-twenties, Synge wrote:

> I was painfully timid, and while still young the idea of Hell took a fearful hold on me. One night I thought I was irretrievably damned and cried myself to sleep in vain yet terrified efforts to form a conception of eternal pain. In the morning I renewed my lamentations and my mother was sent for. She comforted me with the assurance that the Holy Ghost was convicting me of sin and thus preparing me for ultimate salvation. This was a new idea and I rather approved.

Between the ages of four and twenty-one Synge took part in his family's annual move to Greystones in County Wicklow, where his mother had friends and associates among the evangelical community. These 'summer visits to the seaside,' Synge remembered, 'were delightful.' His mother had the policy on holidays as well as during the rest of the year of gathering together as many members of her family as were available. When they were not available in great numbers, she invited friends, usually women of the missionary persuasion, to share the family sojourn in Wicklow, which often lasted for three months.

Nicholas Grene writes about Synge's relationship to his family:

> There is nothing very unusual about a writer or artist from a conventional middle-class background diverging from his family's political, social and religious views. What is striking about Synge's case is that he maintained such close relations with the family in spite of his dissidence.

However, while he spent most of his life in Ireland under his mother's roof, sharing even her holidays, he seems to have been seldom alone with her and this might have helped to maintain close relations. Mrs Synge's house in Orwell Park had an entrance in the dividing wall to her mother's adjoining house, where her daughter Annie, her husband and their children, including the young Edward Stephens, lived, as did Aunt Jane, Mr Synge's sister. On April 13 1890, after Mrs Synge's mother's death, when the Stephens family decided to leave Rathgar, Mrs Synge wrote to her son about her prayers to the Lord:

> I am ... asking Him to find us two houses together as we are here. He can do all things, so if he pleases to do that for me it is quite easy for Him.

The Lord came to her aid. He was assisted by Mr Talbot Coall, the estate agent; they combined to find two adjoining houses at Crosthwaite Park in Kingstown, now Dun Laoghaire. Thus the extended family remained together and Mrs Synge could continue to instruct her grandchildren in the ways of righteousness, as she had her children. While four of her five children carried her instruction faithfully into adulthood, it remained a great sadness to her that John, the youngest, did not. In her letter about the Lord assisting the estate agent, she also wrote: 'Dear Sam [her son who became a missionary to China] is always a comfort when I see him. My poor Johnnie is not a comfort yet.' Soon after the move she wrote:

> John – poor boy. I am so sorry for him, he looks unhappy. He has not found the Saviour yet and until he does, how can he be happy?

Her son, who had not found the Saviour, had found much comfort instead in the natural sciences and in his own imagination. In his autobiographical sketch, he wrote about an awakening which changed everything for him:

> When I was about fourteen I obtained a book of Darwin's. It opened in my hands at a passage where he asks how can we explain the similarity between a man's hand and a bird's or a bat's wings except by evolution. I flung the book aside and rushed out into the open air – it was summer and we were in the country – the sky seemed to have lost its blue and the grass

> its green. I lay down and writhed in an agony of doubt ...
> Incest and parricide were but a consequence of the idea that
> possessed me ... Soon afterwards I turned my attention to
> works of Christian evidence, reading them at first with
> pleasure, soon with doubt, and at last in some cases with
> derision.

Synge was not naturally social. Because of ill-health he had
been educated at home for much of the time. Thus, when he
went to Trinity College in Dublin, he took no great part in
academic or student life. His reading had been intense and
sporadic. His study of science and archaeology had been done
for their own sake. His most notable attribute was his reserve.
By seventeen he did not seem to have shared his doubts and
derisions with his mother who wrote:

> This is Johnnie's birthday. I can hardly fancy he is seventeen. I
> have been looking back to the time he was born. I was so
> dreadfully delicate and he, poor child, was the same ... I see no
> spiritual life in my poor Johnnie; there may be some but it is
> not visible to my eyes. He is very reserved and shut up on the
> subject and if I say anything to him he never answers me, so I
> don't know in the least his state of mind – it is a trying state,
> *very* trying. I long so to be able to see behind that close reserve,
> but I can only wait and pray and hope ...

But it was hopeless. He could not be spoken to about
matters either spiritual or temporal. Within a year, she was
writing again:

> He does not know how to take care of his clothes and won't
> take advice; he has much to learn, poor boy; he is very
> headstrong.

That summer she sent for a clergyman, who discussed
religion with her son in private, leading her son to the view that
he would have to come clean about his unbelief. The Sunday
before Christmas, his mother wrote in her diary: 'Fine, damp,
mild day – church very hot – I felt overpowered. Johnnie
would not come – very sad.' And then on Christmas Day:
'Very peaceful, happy day; went to church – my own sorrow
Johnnie – he did not come.'

Later, Synge wrote:

> Soon after I relinquished the Kingdom of God I began to take
> a real interest in the Kingdom of Ireland. My patriotism went
> round from a vigorous and unreasoning loyalty to a temperate
> nationalism and everything Irish became sacred.

This was a piece of easy subsequent self-positioning, however,
and it is unlikely that a shift in faith as swift and facile as he
suggests actually took place. It is much more likely that his
religious faith, if replaced by anything, was replaced by an
interest in music. As well as attending Trinity, he attended the
Academy of Music in Westland Row where he studied the
violin, becoming one of the many Irish playwrights whose first
love was music. His mother was impressed by his musical
ability. A month before his seventeenth birthday, she wrote:

> Johnnie's ear is wonderfully good now, he hears if the piano is
> at all out of tune … [He] and I play together sometimes … He
> is greatly improved in time; at first he never kept with me and
> still runs *away* when he ought to rest, so I have to try and watch
> him as well as play my own part. We played some nice slow
> melodies last night, and it sounded wonderfully nice.

In these letters, written to her son Robert who was in
Argentina, she compared her two youngest sons.

> Johnnie certainly is the literary man of the family. I never saw
> such a love of reading as he has – he would spend any amount
> of money on books if he had it … I think Johnnie takes after
> my father.

Sam, on the other hand, 'can't help being slow. He is very like
his dear father in that as well as other things.' Sam followed his
mother in religion 'and his virtues make him a comfort to me'.
Yet John, who his mother believed had 'a good opinion of
himself', which she thought a pity, impressed her in ways
which might have mattered to her more and which she could
not take for granted. Although his lack of religion made her
sad, mother and son did not fall out and he was included in all
family events and outings, the silent, stubborn dissenter at the
table. Nonetheless, she lamented his state of ungrace year after
year, in letter after letter; she was the only keener of the eastern

seaboard. 'Oh! My dear Johnnie is a great sorrow to my heart,' she wrote in 1896 when he was twenty-five,

> his belief or mis-belief has no joy in it and his residence abroad
> has been no help to him – he is wonderfully separate from us. I
> show him all the love I can. I pity him so much and love him
> so deeply – and I believe God is hearing my cry to Him, but
> the answer is delayed long. If we are all taken up to meet the
> Lord and he is left behind – how sad a thought but I won't
> think that – God can do all things – so I say to my doubts 'be
> gone …'

Synge's Aunt Jane, who lived in the extended household, had often dandled the young Parnell on her knee when they were neighbours in Wicklow; she now 'piously wished she had choked him in infancy', as W.J. McCormack put it in his biography of Synge, *The Fool of the Family*. The Synges were staunch defenders of the union and it is not hard to imagine their horror at the growing involvement of Synge in cultural nationalism. While his mother disapproved of his interest in archaeology, she did not object, however, to his studying Irish at Trinity College. He took Irish with Hebrew, and these were seen as part of the Divinity Course, Irish being useful to those who wished to convert the native speakers of the West of Ireland to the reformed faith. His Aunt Jane remembered how her brother Alexander, who had ministered on the Aran Islands, had also learned Irish. Like Lady Gregory who began to study Irish in these years, Synge and his fellow students used an Irish translation of the Bible to help them. Like Lady Gregory too, some magic came to Synge from the language he was learning, or some set of emotions which were part of that decade. Both he and Lady Gregory, in the same years and through the same influences, slowly began to love Ireland, as though Ireland were a person. They loved its landscape and its ancient culture; they loved the ordinary people they met in cabins or on the roads. It was as though their own dying power in Ireland, the faded glory of their class, gave their emotions about Ireland a strange glow of intensity. They were both slow to turn this new emotion into politics. As Nicholas Grene has pointed out:

Synge canvassed for an Anti-Home Rule Petition in 1893 and
as late as 1895 was of the view that Home Rule would provoke
sectarian conflict.

So too in 1893, Lady Gregory published anonymously a
pamphlet called *Home Ruin*, essentially a piece of pro-unionist
rhetoric. Slowly, however, they both realized that their project,
if not political, was bound up with politics. Synge would later
write: 'Patriotism gratifies man's need for adoration and has,
therefore, a peculiar power upon the imaginative sceptic.' And
also:

> The Irish country rains, mists, pale insular skies, the old
> churches, manuscripts, jewels, everything in fact that was Irish
> had a charm neither human nor divine, rather perhaps as if I
> had fallen in love with a goddess.

The goddess came in many guises; flirting with her in these
years between the fall of Parnell and independence forced Lady
Gregory and Synge and others to deal in vast ambiguities, to
turn a blind eye to the irony of their own position. Lady
Gregory collected her rents at Coole from the same people
from whom she collected folklore and with some of the same
zeal. When they did not pay, she threatened them. W.J.
McCormack writes in his biography:

> As early as 1885, Synge's brother had been active as an agent,
> and in 1887 his services had been employed to dispossess
> tenants on the Glanmore estate in County Wicklow in an
> incident reported in the Freeman's Journal. According to the
> dramatist's nephew, 'when Synge argued with his mother over
> the rights of tenants and the injustice of evicting them, her
> answer was 'What would become of us if our tenants in
> Galway stopped paying their rents?'

When Synge was twenty-one his mother altered her summer
routine, exchanging Greystones for the interior of County
Wicklow. The fact that the house she rented was boycotted did
not seem to bother her, or prevent Synge from going with her.
He read *Diarmuid and Grainne* that first summer in the
boycotted house and began to explore Wicklow with enormous
enthusiasm. But, according to Edward Stephens:

they were not allowed to forget that they were staying in a
boycotted house. In the evenings sometimes two constables
came up the avenue and walked around the outbuildings to see
that all was well.

In 1895 when that house was not available, they rented Duff
House on Lough Dan, but, as Edward Stephens wrote:

> It was with some misgivings that Mrs Synge brought her future
> daughter-in-law there, for as the house was owned by Roman
> Catholics, she feared it would not be free from fleas.

Synge's writings about Wicklow, eight articles in all, represent
in W.J. McCormack's phrase 'a psychopathology of County
Wicklow'. He loved the idea of tramps and vagrants and saw
his own class as doomed. 'In this garden,' he wrote,

> one seemed to feel the tragedy of the landlord class ... and of
> the innumerable old families that are quickly dwindling away
> ... The broken green-houses and mouse-eaten libraries, that
> were designed and collected by men who voted with Grattan,
> are perhaps as mournful in the end as the four mud walls that
> are so often left in Wicklow as the only remnants of a
> farmhouse ... Many of the descendants of these people have,
> of course, drifted into professional life in Dublin, or have gone
> abroad; yet, wherever they are, they do not equal their
> forefathers.

In one of the essays, as Nicholas Grene has discovered, he
wrote and then omitted 'his most telling condemnation of his
own class':

> Still, this class, with its many genuine qualities, had little
> patriotism, in the right sense, few ideas, and no seed for future
> life, so it has gone to the wall.

Synge wondered what use such a decaying class could be to a
playwright:

> If a playwright chose to go through the Irish country houses he
> would find material, it is likely, for many gloomy plays that
> would turn on the dying away of the old families, and on the
> lives of the one or two delicate girls that are left so often to
> represent a dozen hearty men who were alive a generation or
> two ago.

His problem, as these ideas began to formulate in his mind, was his lack of worldly ambition. He wanted to be a musician. When his brother-in-law advised against it, his advice had not 'the least effect'. Robert, his brother, returned from Argentina and now a land agent, offered to take Synge into his office and train him to become a land agent too. This did not meet with any enthusiasm. His cousin Mary Synge, who was a professional musician, came to stay and advised him to go to Germany to study music. His mother agreed to pay. At the end of July 1893 he left for Coblenz, where he lodged with a family of four sisters whose company he loved, as he loved the company of most women. He stayed in Germany for almost a year, coming home in time to join his mother and the rest of their family for their annual sojourn in County Wicklow.

That summer he renewed an acquaintance with Cherrie Matheson, a neighbour in Kingstown who came to stay with the Synges in Wicklow. His falling in love with her served to emphasize his own marginal position in his class. He had no prospects, just as he had no religion. Nonetheless, he wanted to marry her as he returned to Germany in October and from there, in January 1895, he went to live in Paris where he remained until the end of June, teaching English, attending lectures in the Sorbonne and idling with others of his kind in the city. That summer and winter in Dublin were filled with his obsession with Cherrie, whom he saw a great deal. At the beginning of 1896 he returned to Paris. 'He had left the woman he idealized,' Edward Stephens wrote,

> and had refused to engage in any money-making occupation which might have enabled him to offer her a home. He was going to Paris and to Rome with a general plan for studying languages and literature, inspired by the hope of developing his own productive powers in a way which, as yet, he could picture but dimly.

After three months in Rome, he returned to Paris from where he wrote to Cherrie proposing marriage. When she refused, he wrote to his mother. Her diary entry reads: 'I got a sad *sad* letter from my poor Johnnie in Paris.' He returned to Ireland, and soon began to see Cherrie once more. She remembered:

> Sometimes we went to the National Gallery or some picture exhibition, sometimes to sit for an hour in St Patrick's Cathedral and just drink in the beauty of the dear old place … He liked that part of Dublin more than the modern part and especially Patrick's Street, which runs between the two Cathedrals, and was then more like some queer continental street with little booths all down the centre of it.

Synge did not live long enough to reposition himself in a set of memoirs. It was clear, however, from his preface to *The Playboy of the Western World*, that he would, had he lived, have easily joined Yeats, Lady Gregory, Sean O'Casey and many others in doing so. He wrote:

> When I was writing *The Shadow of the Glen*, some years ago, I got more aid than any learning could have given me, from a chink in the floor of the old Wicklow house where I was staying, that let me hear what was being said by the servant girls in the kitchen.

This suggested that the girls were native Irish rural girls, proto-Pegeen Mikes. As Nicholas Grene has pointed out,

> they were Ellen the cook and Florence Massey the maid, both of whom had been brought up in a Protestant orphanage and did not necessarily come from Wicklow at all.

Yeats outlived Synge by thirty years; Lady Gregory outlived him by twenty-three, and they both created versions of him which suited them. In the years when the three of them worked together, there was a strange hostility lurking in the shadows while centre stage stood solidarity, mutual support and kindness. It was as though both Yeats and Lady Gregory harboured the view that Synge was on the verge of finding them out as they shifted ground and reinvented themselves in the early years of the twentieth century.

There was also the small issue of class. In his essay 'Good Behaviour: Yeats, Synge and Anglo-Irish Etiquette', Roy Foster pondered the relationship between Yeats and Synge when they first met in Paris in 1896, when Yeats was thirty-one and Synge twenty-five. 'Yeats's background was an important notch or two down that carefully defined ladder,' Foster wrote.

> Synge's ancestors were bishops, while Yeats's were rectors; Synge's had established huge estates and mock castles, while Yeats's drew the rent from small farms and lived in the Dublin suburbs. Yeats had no money, while Synge had a small private income. Yeats had no university education, whereas Synge had been to Trinity ... Another important difference between them, which reflects upon background and education, is that Synge, for all his unpretentiousness, was really cosmopolitan; whereas Yeats when they met, was desperately trying to be.

Yeats had had bohemianism foisted upon him by his feckless father; Synge had done it all alone as a new way of killing his mother. Yeats later described their first meeting:

> He told me that he had been living in France and Germany, reading French and German literature, and that he wished to become a writer. He had, however, nothing to show but one or two poems and impressionistic essays, full of that morbidity that has its root in too much brooding over methods of expression, and ways of looking at life, which come, not out of life, but out of literature, images reflected from mirror to mirror ... life had cast no light upon his writings. He had learned Irish years ago, but had begun to forget it, for the only literature that interested him was that conventional language of modern poetry which had begun to make us all weary ... I said 'Give up Paris. You will never create anything by reading Racine, and Arthur Symons will always be a better critic of French literature. Go to the Aran Islands. Live there as if you were one of the people themselves; express a life that has never found expression.'

Yeats wrote this account of their conversations in Paris in 1905, claiming that they had taken place six years earlier, whereas they had taken place nine years before, shortly after Yeats's own first visit to the Aran Islands. Declan Kiberd in *Synge and the Irish Language* and Roy Foster, however, have pointed out more essential inaccuracies in what became, for many years, the standard account of Synge's impulse to go to the Islands. Synge, through his study of the Breton language and his meeting with the Celtic scholar Richard Best, had been taking an intense interest in Celtic Studies in Paris in any case, as Declan Kiberd has emphasized. He knew about the Islands because his uncle had been a minister there. 'Doubtless,' Kiberd has written,

> the advice from Yeats was an important factor in Synge's decision; but the passionate studies in Breton culture must have awakened his enthusiasm for the Gaelic lore of his own country, to which he already held the key in his knowledge of the Irish language. It would be naïve to follow Greene and Stephens [Synge's biographers] in asserting that he went to Aran at Yeats's suggestion. He was heading in that direction from the very beginning.

He wrote to his mother in Dublin about his new friends in Paris who included Yeats and Maud Gonne. (One of his friends later reported that 'Synge gently hated Miss Gonne.') He explained that he had become interested in socialism, which his mother thought 'utter folly'. He became a member of the committee of Maud Gonne's Irish League, but politics did not interest him as much as culture, and he resigned after a few months. In the summer of 1897, despite his cosmopolitanism and his new friends, he returned to Ireland so he could go to Wicklow on holidays with his mother. That summer, as he became ill, his hair falling out and a lump developing on his neck, some of his family put it down to unrequited love. But it was the beginning of the Hodgkin's disease that would kill him twelve years later. His mother wrote:

> Johnnie is at home still. He has to get those large glands taken out of his neck, poor fellow. It is very unpleasant ... Since his hair fell out he got cold in the glands, and they became so large they were, or rather are, quite disfiguring to him. He has been very anxious to go away to Paris. He has been advised by his friend Yeats, the Irish poet, to go in for reviewing French literature so John is working away with that end in view. His general health is very good and he is strong and able to walk, so I trust he may get over this time well, please God, and Oh I do ask Him to reveal Himself to my dear boy.

It is interesting that there is no mention here of the Aran Islands. The operation took place in December 1897. The doctors must have known that the symptoms could recur, but they told Synge and his mother, who both seemed to have believed them, that it was a success. His mother watched over him. On 3 January 1898 she noted in her diary: 'John not well – made me anxious.' Two days later she wrote to her son Robert:

> Johnnie looks much better, but he is not strong, and I am anxious lest he should go to Paris too soon and be laid up again in some way, as the Hotel life is anything but comfortable or healthy. He is very silent, poor fellow, and spends all his time over his books except when he goes out for a walk.

When he went back to Paris, writing fragmentary beginnings to a novel and attending lectures by a French professor on the connections between Irish and Greek literature, his mother wrote: 'I heard from Johnnie; troubled by bugs.'

On 23 April 1898 he came home. The difference between his life in Paris, where he spoke fluent French, lived alone and was deeply respected by his many associates, and his life in his mother's house, must have made him wonder. At least three times a day for meals in Ireland he had to listen to Mrs Synge and her friends and other members of the family on the subject of religion and domestic life and their narrow political prejudices. She was teaching her grandchildren the Bible as she had taught her children, seeing it as part of her duty, according to Edward Stephens, to emphasize the horror of eternal damnation. 'Sometimes,' Stephens wrote,

> our lessons were interrupted by his [Synge's] entering the room. I remember particularly his coming in once when we were having a Bible reading. He was twirling his pocket scissors on his finger chanting softly to himself, 'Holy, Holy, Holy Moses.' We greeted him and he sat in the window for a few minutes and then, feeling that he had caused an interruption, went quietly out again. Our grandmother said: 'Don't put down your Bibles when Uncle John comes in,' and resumed her reading.

In Paris, he was the earnest playboy of the western world; in Kingstown he was his mother's youngest son.

Just before Synge's first visit to the Aran Islands, he had two final meetings with Cherrie Matheson, who told him that

their differences were irreconcilable. Two days later, he called
to her house and had what must have been a deeply dispiriting
conversation with Cherrie and her mother. Mrs Matheson,
according to Edward Stephens,

> with Cherrie's approval, rated him soundly for pressing a
> rejected proposal of marriage when he was not earning enough
> money to support himself. He left in despair … His mind was
> still distraught with anguish when, on the morning of Monday
> 9 May 1898, he left by the morning train for Galway.

He wrote of his visits to the Islands over the next few years
with beauty and reverence and restraint. It must have been a
relief that first morning watching the sailors casting off in a fog
from Galway pier and arriving in Aranmore after a three-hour
journey, no one there knowing anything about Cherrie
Matheson and her hectoring mother, or Mrs Synge's worries
about her poor Johnnie. He was now in the land of his dreams.
Lady Gregory saw him on the island in 1898; she was in search,
too, of nourishment from a primitive world which contained
an astonishing life force and an ancient culture. She wrote:

> I first saw him in the North Island of Aran. I was staying there,
> gathering folklore, talking to the people, and felt a real pang of
> indignation when I passed another outsider walking here and
> there, talking also to the people. I was jealous of not being
> alone on the island among the fishers and the seaweed
> gatherers. I did not speak to the stranger nor was he inclined to
> speak to me. He also looked on me as an intruder.

Later, she wrote about his work once he had arrived on the
Islands:

> He had done no good work until he came back to his own
> country. It was there that he found all he wanted, fable,
> emotion, style … bringing a cultured mind to a mass of
> primitive material, putting clearer and lasting form to the
> clumsily expressed emotion of a whole countryside.

Soon, he was invited to Coole and quickly became part of
the movement which resulted in the Abbey Theatre. He
became, eventually, with Yeats and Lady Gregory, one of the
three directors. He wrote five plays for them – *The Shadow of the*

Glen (1903); *Riders to the Sea* (1904); *The Well of the Saints* (1905) *The Tinker's Wedding* (1907); *The Playboy of the Western World* (1907). He left one play unfinished, *Deirdre of the Sorrows*, which was first produced, in a completed version, in 1910. His imagination was powerfully autonomous; his plays combined the knowledge he had amassed through his study and his wanderings in Europe with a real openness and freedom and an immense natural talent. He delighted in language and character, in wild talk and massive abandon, as though he were concerned to dramatize and most portray what he himself in his own life kept in abeyance.

In these eleven years he took part in all the rows which ran at the theatre, seeming much of the time calmer, more focused, less vindictive and, on some matters, more determined than his colleagues. He believed that Yeats was too impetuous to deal with the actors. In some of the correspondence, as Roy Foster has pointed out, 'he sounds both older and wiser than Yeats; he appears more at ease in dealing with people.' In 1908, when the Fays had left the theatre Synge remarked: 'Since then Yeats and I have been running the show, i.e. Yeats looks after the stars and I do the rest.' The actors and workers in the theatre liked him. He appeared more natural, more in possession of himself than either of his colleagues. An Australian visitor in 1904 described him:

> He was full of race and good breeding, courteous, sensitive, sincere … a simple man; but there was something strange and alluring about him, an indescribable charm expressed in his voice and manner and, above all, in his curious smile that was at the same time ironic and sympathetic.

With the Abbey, as with his family, Synge was skilled at withdrawing. 'I have often envied him his absorption,' Yeats wrote, 'as I have envied Verlaine his vice.'

Lady Gregory disliked *The Playboy of the Western World*, although she defended it in public. She made sure that Yeats's play *The Pot of Broth* was not used as a curtain-raiser, which would be, she wrote to Yeats, foreseeing the riots, like 'Synge setting fire to your house to roast his own pig.' After Synge's

death, she wrote a passage in her journal which she did not
publish:

> One doesn't want a series of panegyrics and we can't say, don't
> want to say what was true, he was ungracious to his fellow
> workers, authors and actors, ready in accepting praise, grudging
> in giving it … On tour he thought of his own play only, gave
> no help to ours and if he repeated compliments, they were to
> his own.'

Yeats in his journal wrote: 'I never heard him praise any
writer, living or dead, but some old French farce-writer.'

The truth was that he understood the value of his own plays
and did not rate very highly the work of Yeats or Lady Gregory
for the theatre, although he admired other aspects of their
work, such as Lady Gregory's translations. He made no secret
of this, and of his profound irritation at Lady Gregory's tireless
and fearless promotion of Yeats's work and her constant
production of her own work. In December 1906 she told
Synge that Yeats's dramatic work 'was more important than
any other (you must not be offended at this) as I think it our
chief distinction.' In March 1907, when *The Playboy of the
Western World* has already been produced and Charles Frohman,
an American producer, came to the Abbey looking for new
work to tour in the U.S., Synge wrote to Molly Allgood:

> I hear that they are showing Frohman *one* play of mine,
> 'Riders', five or six of L.G.'s [Lady Gregory's] and several of
> Yeats. I am raging about it, though of course you must not
> breathe a word about it. I suppose after the P.B. [*Playboy*] fuss
> they are afraid of stirring up the Irish Americans if they take
> me. However I am going to find out what is at the bottom of it
> and if I am not getting fair play I'll withdraw my plays from
> both tours English and American altogether. It is getting past a
> joke the way they are treating me.

They, on the other hand, became increasingly sure that they
had invented him. After his death Lady Gregory wrote to
Yeats:

> You did more than anyone for him, you gave him a means of
> expression. You have given me mine, but I should have found
> something else to do, though not anything coming near this,

but I don't think Synge would have done anything but drift but
for you and the theatre ... I think you and I supplied him with
vitality when he was with us as the wild people did in the
Blaskets.

As soon as Synge arrived on the Aran Islands, he wrote to
his mother, who wrote to his brother Sam:

> I had a very interesting letter from Johnnie last week ... The
> islanders of Aran found out that he was related to Uncle Aleck
> [who had been a missionary on the Islands] and came to see
> him and were quite pleased. He is now on Inishmaan Island –
> went there in a *curragh* and is much pleased with his new abode,
> a room in a cottage inside the kitchen of a house ... and he
> lives on mackerel and eggs and learns Irish; how wonderfully
> he accommodates himself to his various surroundings.

When he returned to Dublin he accommodated himself to
his mother's surroundings once more, joining her on holiday in
County Wicklow. He would return to the family from his daily
outings by foot or bicycle with stories of tramps he had met,
including one who claimed to have known his grandmother
and who had told him: 'I never went there but Mrs Synge
offered me a glass of whisky.' Later, when the young Edward
Stephens mentioned the tramp to Synge's mother, she
remarked:

> I wish Uncle Johnnie would not encourage tramps; I don't
> know why he wants to talk to queer people. I'm sure that Mrs
> Synge never offered a tramp whisky.

Once the summer was over, Synge followed his usual
routine. He returned to Paris for the winter, visiting Brittany in
the spring and returning to Ireland for the annual long holiday
with his mother in County Wicklow. This year his mother had
two young women, both interested in evangelical
Protestantism, staying. Synge became close to them. His
mother wrote:

> Both girls are very lively and there is a great deal of joking and
> fun goes on between them and John. I have not see him laugh
> so much for years.

Edward Stephens remembered:

John had learned to enjoy their company so much that he
never withdrew to read in his room when he had an
opportunity of sitting with them on the steps looking at the
view or, on wet days, on camp stools in the porch looking into
the mist that hid everything but the tops of the trees below the
house.

In September Synge returned to the Islands and then in
November to Paris where he began to write his book about the
Aran Islands. In May 1900 he returned once more not to miss
his three months in Wicklow with his mother, who once more
had invited young women, including one Rosie Calthrop, to
stay and keep her son company much to his delight. His
mother, however, became jealous that summer of her son
paying kinder attention to other women than to her. She was
not, it seems, content to play the Widow Quin to her guest's
Pegeen Mike. She wrote to her son Sam:

> She seemed to appreciate Johnnie's thoughtfulness and
> kindness very much! It is a pity he does not show it to me and
> not only to strangers. He was most attentive to both in little
> matters I could see, and he was always at their beck and call to
> walk or ride or escort them anywhere! So no wonder they like
> him, but it was rather aggravating to me; he wanted to put me
> aside entirely. But I told Rosie and then she did not fall in with
> his plans, though she loved to be out walking with him I know.

The idea of Mrs Synge telling her guest that she was jealous
of her son's attention to the guest is intriguing. It is hard to
imagine what terms she used to make herself clear. It is also
possible that the guest was forced to explain to Synge what the
problem was, that the older woman was aggravated by his
sudden success with strangers, and when there were no
strangers around he did not bother displaying his charm and
his willingness to please. Thus a central part of the action of
The Playboy of the Western World was being played out in a rented
house in Wicklow in the summer of 1900.

That September Synge set out again to charm strangers by
returning to the Aran Islands. This was his third visit. He
arrived in a particular state of gloom because his neighbour
Cherrie Matheson had been receiving a gentleman whom she

would later marry. They had met on the street and Cherrie had introduced her new boyfriend to Synge. The following month when he returned, this visit having sown the seeds that would become *Riders to the Sea*, his mother wrote to his brother Sam:

> Johnnie came home last night from the Aran Islands. He has one very large gland on his neck just above his collar; he looks very well and the time on the Islands agreed with him. I was glad to have him safe back. The sea has been very rough and great gales lately and it was hard for him to get away. He had a very rough passage to Galway on a miserable little steamer. The engines stopped several times and went on again.

That autumn Synge bought a portable typewriter, a Blickensdorfer, which Richard Best chose for him. It came in a varnished wooden case. When he brought it home, he said that it spelt worse than he did. When he went back to Paris, his mother missed him. She wrote to Sam:

> My poor Johnnie went off this morning; it is very calm, I am thankful to say, but raining and thick at sea … I miss Johnnie. As usual I have been very busy stitching and mending his clothes and getting him some new ones. The gland on his neck is very large, but back pretty far. He is getting rather anxious about it. I think he is improved; he has been more pleasant and chatty than usual of late, and I think his queer time in Paris always injures him, and he is so queer when he comes home and so out of all our ways, and then it wears off by degrees. I am trying to persuade him to give up his room in Paris and make a fresh start nearer home.

The gland in his neck was still swollen when he returned at the beginning of the summer; when he saw the doctor in Dublin he was given an ointment and a different medicine. His mother invited Rosie Calthrop to stay with them once more and wrote to Sam about the amount of money Synge and Rosie had spent on an outing. 'John does not mind at all,' she wrote, 'of course it is my money and he has no scruples about that. However, I don't mind now and then, but I would not like it often.' Synge had his typewriter with him and was working on the first draft of a play *When the Moon Has Set*,[1] which dealt with his own class and was thinly disguised autobiography, which he brought with him when he went to stay at Coole. Lady Gregory, when she read the play, told him, however, that it was not good and of no literary interest. From Coole he went west to the Islands and then back to Paris. That May of 1902 he was asked to review Lady Gregory's *Cuchulain of Muirthemne*, in which a version of the dialect spoken around Coole was used. Synge found this dialect close to the living speech he knew from rural Wicklow. In his review he described the language as 'wonderfully simple and powerful ... almost Elizabethan.' The Elizabethan vocabulary, he wrote,

> has a force and colour that make it the only form of English that is quite suitable for incidents of the epic kind, and in her intercourse with the peasants of the West Lady Gregory has learned to use this vocabulary in a new way, while she carries with her plaintive Gaelic constructions that make her language, in a true sense, a language of Ireland.

He was working on the drafts of his first plays. In *The Shadow of the Glen* and *The Tinker's Wedding* he was, to some small extent, dramatizing the role of the artist, or the outsider, versus the role of the settled and respectable community; in other words, he made these plays as versions of his own plight at being turned down by Cherrie Matheson. Other aspects of these plays came from his own dreams and observations, especially in the summer months in Wicklow. Edward Stephens, who was fourteen at the time his uncle worked on these plays, wrote that the material

> was derived from the lore of the country people, not from any direct association with the tinkers themselves. They were so dirty and in their mode of life so disreputable that it would have been impossible for John to mix with them at his ease. He warned me against dropping into conversation with them on the road.

---

[1] The full text of this play, which has not been widely published, is included here, in an edition by Ann Saddlemyer, on p.147.

By the beginning of the October of 1902 Synge had finished both *Riders to the Sea* and *The Shadow of the Glen*. On his way to the Aran Islands for his final visit – his book on the Islands still had not found a publisher – he stopped off at Coole to show the plays to Yeats and Lady Gregory, who described the plays as 'both masterpieces, both perfect in their way.' Later she wrote:

> He had gathered emotion, the driving force he needed from his life among the people, and it was the working in dialect that set free his style.

Yeats saw the language of the Bible as another influence.

Early the following year he decided to give up his room in Paris. When he unpacked his French belongings in Dublin, Edward Stephens watched him taking out

> the knife and fork and little frying pan that he had used in Paris, he showed them to me as if they were things he regarded with affection. I asked him whether they had ever been cleaned, he replied: 'A thing that is used by me only is never dirty.'

Because of attacks of asthma he spent that summer in Kerry rather than in Wicklow, returning to Dublin for the rehearsals of *The Shadow of the Glen*, which opened in October to considerable controversy. When Synge and his mother went down to breakfast the morning after the opening night, they read in *The Irish Times* that the play was 'excessively distasteful' while the critic admitted 'the cleverness of the dialect and the excellent acting of Nora and the tramp.'

Edward Stephens wrote about his grandmother's response to the play:

> All she read in the Irish Times perplexed her. She had thought of John as being overpersuaded by his literary friends into praising everything Irish but, now that a play of his had been acted, the newspapers were censuring him for attacking Irish character. She disliked the kind of publicity his work was getting, she was sorry that he should have adopted a form of dramatic writing that was likely to prove no more remunerative

than the Aran book, and she was sorry that any of his work should be connected with the stage.

Mrs Synge also worried about her son, now aged thirty-two, being out late. She wrote in her diary:

After a dreadful storm last night, I had a headache from lying awake listening to the storm and watching for Johnnie who was not home until 3.30.

The Irish Times had nothing much good to say about *Riders to the Sea* either when the play opened in February 1904. The Synges disapproved of what they read about it. 'The idea underlying the work is good enough,' the critic said,

but the treatment of it is to our mind repulsive. Indeed the play develops into something like a wake. The long exposure of the dead body before an audience may be realistic, but is certainly not artistic. There are some things which are lifelike, and yet are quite unfit for presentation on the stage and we think that *Riders to the Sea* is one of them.

Edward Stephens remembered his father's response: 'If they want an Irish play, why can't they act *The Shaughraun?*'

The plays, however, were much praised by the London critics, but this made no difference to Synge's family who were 'serenely unaware of the importance of his work.' After a sojourn in the West, Synge decided in October 1904 to find his own lodgings in Rathmines and move out of the family home. In January 1905 *The Well of the Saints* went into rehearsal with a walk-on part for a young actress, Molly Allgood, whose sister Sara was a well-known actress. She was nineteen. Soon she began to play important roles in the theatre's repertoire, including Synge's plays.

Both the Synge family and Lady Gregory disapproved of Synge's relationship with Molly, the Synges for religious and social reasons, Lady Gregory because she did not want directors of the theatre consorting too freely with its employees. While he could not keep the relationship a secret from Lady Gregory, Synge could hide it from his mother. On 5 November 1906, when he had moved back into his mother's house and given up his flat, he wrote to Molly: 'My mother asked me again if I was alone, and I said I had "a friend" with me. I must tell her soon.' Seventeen days later, he wrote again:

> I showed my mother your photo the other night and told her you were a great friend of mine. That is as far as I can go until I am stronger. I am thoroughly sick of this state of affairs we must end it, and make ourselves public.

That day, as he was suffering from influenza, Molly came to his mother's house. Later, Synge wrote to her:

> My mother is too shy to say much about you, but I think she is pleased. She said you seemed very bright and she hoped I had asked you to come down on Sunday and cheer me up. I said I hadn't but I would write. Today she has reminded me several times not to forget my note to you.

The following month, when he told his mother he was engaged to Molly, he wrote:

> I heard from my mother. She says she thought 'the friend' I have been walking with was a man, but that my showing her the photo and the letters that came so often when I was ill made her think there was some thing. Then she says it would be a good thing if it would make me happier, and to wind up she points out how poor we shall be with only £100 a year. Quite a nice letter for the first go off. So that is satisfying.

While Synge sent Molly only the good news about his mother's response to his marrying a Catholic, it is easy to read between the lines of his letters. The following March, for example, he remarked that his mother 'is more much rational about it than she was.' This suggests that she had been, in the previous months, irrational in her response. Later that month, she began to enquire in some detail about her future daughter-in-law:

> My mother was enquiring about your temper today, she says my temper is so bad, it would be a terrible thing to marry a bad-tempered wife.

That January, as the rehearsals for *The Playboy of the Western World* started, Synge began to write to Molly about the possibility of finding a flat. Molly was playing Pegeen Mike.

Willie Fay, who was producing, and his brother Frank realized how much indignation the play would provoke:

> Frank and I begged him to make Pegeen a decent likeable country girl, which she might easily have been without injury to the play, and to take out the torture scenes in the last act, where the peasants burn Christy with lit turf ... Frank and I might as well have saved our breath. We might as well have tried to move the Hill of Howth as move Synge.

In her diary, once she had read the *Irish Times* account of the play and the opening night, Mrs Synge recorded: 'I was troubled about John's play – not nice.' Synge himself was troubled by a cough which he could not shake off. In all these years he seemed to be suffering regularly from coughs and colds and other ailments. By April, he was making plans to get married.

> I counted up my money last night and if all goes well I think we shall have £150 for our first year, if we get married soon, that is £3 a week.

In January 1908 he found a flat in York Road in Rathmines for thirteen shillings and sixpence a week. His mother wrote:

> Johnnie is on the move; he is at home today packing and sorting over books, clothes etc. ... I feel his going *very* much: furnishing these rooms, trying to make a little home for himself on such a very small and uncertain income. I am giving him some old furniture etc, and he must buy some ... Johnnie says this move reminds him of his trips to Paris! Counting over his socks etc putting away things he does not want! However, he adds, it is not far.

Both Synge and his mother were ill that winter. Both had operations, and it must have been clear to the doctors that both of them were doomed. In April, Mrs Synge wrote to her son Robert about Synge's marriage, making clear that she must have been, up to recently, opposing it:

> Johnnie came to see me on Friday last; he is seriously thinking of being soon married ... [and] as he is determined ... it is no use opposing him any more and we must only trust that he may get on.

He was, however, too ill to remain in the flat he had dreamed of with Molly for so long. Once his operation was over, he came home to his mother once more: 'We got [his] furniture all back from Rathmines yesterday,' she wrote,

> It was such a sad little flitting altogether. I remember now remarking how ill he looked when he was going away. He says those pains began in December! I think if he had been at home, I would certainly have thought there was something serious going on; but I saw him very seldom during the four months he was away, and I know he did not feed himself as he was accustomed and he used to be so very hungry for his dinners when he came. God has permitted it all to happen so I can say nothing.

In the time that remained to him, Synge travelled to London, returned to Coblenz to stay with the family who had hosted him more than a decade earlier, wrote tender letters almost daily to Molly Allgood and worked on his play 'Deirdre'. Death was never far from his mind. On 2 November 1908 he sent Molly a draft of a new poem:

> I asked if I got sick and died would you
> With my black funeral go walking too,
> If you'd stand close to hear them talk and pray
> While I'm let down in that steep bank of clay.
> And, No, you said, for if you saw a crew
> Of living idiots, pressing round that new
> Oak-Coffin – they alive, I dead beneath
> That board – you'd rave and rend them with your teeth.

His mother died while he was in Germany. On 7 November, on his return to his mother's house where he was to stay for the remaining months of his life, he wrote to Molly: 'I am home at last. I am inexpressibly sad in this empty house.' In February 1909 he went into hospital in the knowledge that he was dying. In his notebooks from his time on the Aran Islands, there is a passage which he did not transcribe fully when he came to write the book. He was on a curragh in a bad sea:

> I thought almost enviously what fatiguing care I would escape
> if the canoe turned a few inches nearer to those waves and

dropped me helpless into the blue bosom of the sea. No death were so delightful. What a difference to die here with the fresh sea saltness in my hair than to struggle in soiled sheets and thick stifling blankets with a smell of my own illness in my nostril and a half paid death tender at my side still my long death battle will be fought out.

During his long death battle, Molly came to see him every day until she went to play Pegeen Mike in Manchester where *The Playboy* was warmly received. On 23 March Yeats wrote to Lady Gregory:

I have just met M. [Molly] in the street and saw by her face that she had bad news. She told me that Synge is now so weak that he cannot raise himself on his arm in bed and at night he can only sleep with the help of drugs. For some days he has been too weak to read. He cannot read even his letters. They have moved him to another room that he may see the mountains from his bed.

The following day he died. He was buried in the family plot in Mount Jerome cemetery. Before the funeral, Synge's brother Robert wrote in his diary: 'Received a visit from Yeats and the Sec. of Abbey Theatre with a request which I refused as impossible.' They wanted to have a death-mask made. Edward Stephens wrote:

Robert would have disliked it under any conditions but he ... believed John's face to have changed so much during his last illness that no real likeness of him ... could have been obtained.

Stephens noticed that at the funeral the mourners were divided, 'as they had always been in his lifetime', between family and the people among whom he had worked. Molly Allgood did not attend his funeral.

Illustration 2: Marie Mullen in the DruidSynge production of *The Tinker's Wedding* (2004). Photograph by Keith Pattison

2 | A Gallous Story and a Dirty Deed: Druid's Synge

Fintan O'Toole

> ... a strange man is a marvel, with his mighty talk; but what's a squabble in your back-yard, and the blow of a loy, have taught me that there's a great gap between a gallous story and a dirty deed. – Pegeen Mike, *The Playboy of the Western World*

It is obvious enough now, but at the time the excitement was too visceral, the surprise too thrilling, for anyone to see it. Initially, Garry Hynes's landmark production of *The Playboy of the Western World*, which took shape over seven years between 1975 and 1982 stood out for what it was not: not soft, not romantic, not redolent of what W.B. Yeats, in an entirely different context, called 'the stale odour of spilt poetry'. It was, above all, not the Abbey. The lush and languid had been replaced with the raw and immediate. Sex hung in the air and dirt clung to the floor. The Widow Quin was hungry for a man's body. Christy picked the caked mud from his bare feet. You could almost put your finger into the gaping gash on Old Mahon's head. When Pegeen went to burn Christy's leg with a sod from the fire, you knew that if it touched his flesh, it would corrode all the way to the bone. The *Playboy*, in other words, was not a classic revival, but a new play and a whole new ball game.

It wasn't just that we hadn't seen Synge like this before, but that we had barely seen him at all. Synge's impact beyond Ireland had been evident from time to time, in Mustapha Matura's 1950 transposition of *The Playboy* to Trinidad, *The Playboy of the West Indies*, or Bertolt Brecht's 1937 play *Señora Carrar's Rifles* which adapts *Riders to the Sea* to the Spanish Civil War. But this idea of Synge as a great contemporary figure scarcely existed in Ireland in the 1970s. The context for Druid's *Playboy* was one in which Synge was a famous but little produced playwright. He did not occupy the world stage. The world saw Synge as Ireland's property, and Ireland saw him as the Abbey's. But even at the Abbey, the real extent of Synge's importance never quite matched the general perception.

Between 1907, when it was first produced, and 1966 *The Playboy* had 249 performances at the Abbey – just two more in total than George Shiels's comedy *Professor Tim*, which was first produced in 1935. *The Shadow of the Glen* had 239 performances in 63 years – just 23 more than Frank Carney's potboiler *The Righteous Are Bold* had in 20 years. (An incidental mark of the relative neglect of Synge is that no one is even sure of the title of the play, which appears in printed editions and in theatre programmes as both *The Shadow of the Glen* and *In the Shadow of the Glen*.) Between 1950 and 1970, Synge had been represented on the Abbey stage only by a 1960 staging of *Riders to the Sea*. *The Tinker's Wedding* remained unperformed at the Abbey until the year of Synge's centenary celebrations in 1971. (It was first staged in Ireland just eight years earlier, at the Pike Theatre, as part of the 1963 Dublin Theatre Festival.) When Eric Bentley directed at the Abbey in 1950, he was told by Ernest Blythe that Synge 'emptied the theatre for five years'.

The other national cultural institution, RTE television, had made *The Well of the Saints* its second-ever drama production in 1962, but then lost interest. There was a production of *The Shadow of the Glen* in 1964, after which the station never again broadcast a Synge play. Synge existed in the worst kind of artistic limbo. He was a semi-official figure, paid too much empty homage as a national treasure to be interesting to the young and yet too neglected to be a real, serious presence in the culture.

This context meant that what was most revealing about Druid's *Playboy* in the late 1970s and early 1980s was what is now most obvious. It told us that Synge is a great playwright and that *The Playboy* is arguably the greatest comedy in the English language since the 17th century. It announced that someone who had seemed defunct was riotously alive. And that was more than enough to be going on with. Only in retrospect can we ask what it was that made that production, and not just the play itself, a great work of art.

Synge himself had an emphatic approach to such a question. He believed that greatness is a matter of resonance, of the way the individual expresses the general. This belief, indeed, is what made him a playwright. Theatre is a public form, one that requires its audience for its completion. Time and place, the here and now, are bred into its bones. In the late 1890s he noted for himself that

> Goethe's weakness [is] due to his having no national and intellectual mood to interpret. The individual mood is often trivial, perverse, fleeting, [but the] national mood [is] broad, serious, provisionally permanent … each work of art must have been possible to only one man at one period and in one place … the great artist, as Rembrandt or Shakespeare, adds his personal distinction to a great distinction of time and place.

In another note, he added that

> No personal originality is enough to make a rich work unique, unless it has also the characteristic of a particular [time] and locality and the life that is in it.

What was the national mood of Ireland in the late 1970s and early 1980s? What was characteristic of that time and place? Many things, of course, but one overarching sensation was the starkness of the space that separated rhetoric from reality, words and their referents, what we said from what we did. This was a period of transition, when the emptiness of inherited rhetorical systems was increasingly apparent, but those systems still held sway. While social realities were

changing and official ideologies were slipping inexorably into
crisis, the old languages of nation, church and state were, if
anything, given a new urgency by a sense of panic.
Conservative Catholicism was rallying in the last ditch, its
apparent revival indicated by events like the visit of Pope John
Paul II in 1979 and the successful campaign for a constitutional
amendment banning abortion. Charles Haughey came to power
as Taoiseach and set about obscuring his own divisiveness by
refurbishing the old rhetoric of national unity. The conflict in
Northern Ireland, which itself had revived the traditional
rhetoric of Irish nationalism, was entering a new phase of
highly-wrought, and self-consciously theatrical symbolism with
the dirty protests and hunger strikes by IRA and INLA
prisoners in the H-Blocks.

Yet all of these attempts at recreating an old language of
inherited certainties were in fact symptoms, not of revival, but
of decline. The authority of the Church was slipping away. The
economy was in decline. Mass emigration was starting up again
and would continue to such an extent that the population of
the Republic actually declined in the 1980s. Stable government
become almost impossible: in 1981 and 1982 alone, there were
three general elections in the Republic. And while the rhetoric
was being ratcheted up, while words were uttered at an ever-
higher pitch, the body was intruding with a strange, sometimes
grotesque insistence. As the body politic wasted away, the body
itself became a bizarre obsession. One set of images that
dominated the island in 1981 and 1982 was the harrowing, pre-
historic figures of unkempt men with long hair and long
beards, each wearing nothing but the blanket that covered a
naked, dwindling body. These spectres haunted Ireland like
emanations from some collective nightmare. And alongside
them were the spectral body parts of women. As the abortion
debate took hold in the early years of the 1980s, wombs, eggs,
sperm, periods, embryos, ectopic pregnancies and ovaries
became the terms of political debate.

This contrast between mighty talk and backyard squabbles,
between gallous stories and dirty deeds, between language and
the body, was played out, above all, in the violence of the

Northern conflict. From day to day, large verbal abstractions –
United Kingdom, United Ireland – were boiled down to dirty
deeds and broken bodies. The great gap between what was said
and what was done was a ditch filled with torn flesh and
shattered bones.

It is striking that John Synge was one of the figures to
whom those in power appealed in their efforts to occlude this
crisis and to re-assert, in the face of its disintegration, the
fundamental stability of their Ireland. In his last major speech
before becoming Taoiseach, a speech that was a key part of his
pitch for the leadership of Fianna Fail, Haughey actually cited
the controversy over *The Playboy* in 1907, fusing, as it were,
Patrick Pearse and John Synge into a single embodiment of the
sophisticated, modern nationalism that he himself claimed to
represent. Pearse, he said,

> was a man of far-ranging literary sympathies. It is a matter of
> historical fact that among the national intellectuals of the
> time, he defended the right of the Abbey to produce *The
> Playboy* and the inalienable right of men of genius to portray
> Irish life as they saw it.

(The claim is significant because it is so disingenuous. Though
Pearse later changed his mind, he condemned Synge at the time
of the *Playboy* riots as a blasphemer 'against the moral order of
the universe', the preacher of 'a sinister and unholy gospel', and
an 'Evil Spirit' who 'railed obscenely against light and
sweetness'.

A year before the classic 1982 Druid production of *The
Playboy*, Haughey again recruited Synge to his own brand of
nationalist cultural conservatism. Speaking of the Blasket
Islands (one of which, of course, he owned), Haughey told the
Royal Irish Academy in March 1981 that

> Synge went there, as did many other scholars and literary men,
> and found that they provided a special link with the
> immemorial past of Ireland and the Irish people.

Haughey's Synge was the icon of an imagined cultural
continuity, a Protestant who had understood that the real
Ireland was to be found in an untouched and sacred West:

> John Millington Synge and his generation set, as many artists
> still do, a special value on all those things which connected us
> with Ireland's past, and they found them in the remote but
> beautiful and tradition-rich places of the West, where the
> language and lore of an ancient people lived on. It is right for
> any country to value this sort of unbroken continuity in its
> experience.

Haughey linked Synge's alleged search for the immemorial
Ireland with his own programme for 'preserving' conservative
values which were imagined as similarly timeless. The Irish, he
claimed, were almost uniquely devoted to the past: 'there is
scarcely any other people who emotionally are so attached to
their inheritance.'

Druid's production of *The Playboy* can be seen in retrospect
as a demolition of Haughey's official version of Synge, with its
age-old continuities, its static, idealized West of Ireland and its
attempt to turn the man who could write that 'every healthy
mind is more interested in Tit Bits than in Idylls of the King'
into a romantic antiquarian. But it was not, of course, a
primarily political statement. While it would be patronizing to
imagine that Garry Hynes and the actors and designers were
unaware of the political resonance of what they were doing,
they were concerned, first and foremost, with the making of a
piece of theatre. It so happened, however, that Druid's
explorations of ways of making theatre concerned the same
things that informed both the public mood of the time and
Synge himself: the gap between language and the body,
between what is said and what is done.

Before Garry Hynes, Synge's plays were magnificent verbal
constructs, whose poetry was to be digested and relished, but
whose literary density placed them at odds with modernist
theatre. When Shelagh Richards produced *The Tinker's Wedding*
in Salzburg in 1949 – presumably the first production by an
Irish director – Eric Bentley, watching the rehearsals, was
fascinated by the way the play was approached as a purely
linguistic artefact:

> Miss Richards stands in direct opposition to the fashionable
> directors of the moment in that she does not believe in the
> predominance of the *mise-en-scène*. The bulk of her attention in
> rehearsals goes to the rendering of the lines, phrase by phrase,
> word by word.

But even the sympathetic Bentley tended towards the
conclusion that this elaborate, highly-tuned language meant
that Synge was too good for this world:

> Even given a correct and eloquent speaking of the lines,
> Synge's Ireland is not easily rendered in the dingy naturalistic
> peepshow of the urban stage.

Druid's Synge was never about neglecting or marginalizing the
spoken word, but it was rooted in a belief that the plays were
not, after all, too delicate for the peepshow of the urban stage.
The company evolved in its early years through its Synge
productions: *The Playboy* in 1975, *The Shadow of the Glen* and *The
Tinker's Wedding* in 1976, *The Playboy* again in 1977 and 1982.
Garry Hynes and the actors had tested Synge's texts in
performance, and had approached them from a variety of
angles. By the time of the 1982 production, Marie Mullen who
played the Widow Quin, had already played Pegeen Mike. Mick
Lally, who played Old Mahon, had already played Christy.
These key actors thus knew the roles that, at times, they were
playing against. There was a depth of involvement, an ease with
the language, that created a confidence in the sheer theatricality
of the plays.

But alongside that journey, there was also an exploration of
the non-verbal elements of theatre, and in particular of the way
they could co-exist with a dense text. The Druid production of
Hynes's own play *Island Protected by a Bridge of Glass* in 1981 can
be seen in retrospect as a testing ground for the physical and
visual expressiveness that would go into the making of an
achieved Druid style of playing Synge. At the time, reviewing it
for *In Dublin*, I was stunned by the sheer variety of techniques
brought to bear on the play:

> Druid raid every available cupboard for the elements of the
> drama. Use is made of the sparse, rapid flow of language into

space of Beckett (Not I comes particularly to mind at times),
the comic representation of ideas by objects and the caricatures
of agitprop farce, the folk rhythms and stylized dance of
Siamsa, mime, and the marvellous music of De Danann. At
times, the imaginative simplicity of Garry Hynes's use of
objects such as long sticks is startling and the energy created by
the quick succession of forms and methods is irresistible.

This was not simply a matter of testing the ways in which
words and images could work together, however. It was also
about figuring out how they could work against each other. For
Hynes's mature approach to Synge, as it emerged in the 1982
Playboy, overturned all notions of him as a figure of continuity
who represents an archaic, unified world. It enacted, rather, the
electrifying tensions and the coiled-up contradictions within
the world he presents. We heard the beauty of the language,
enhanced by the fluency of actors who understand it, but we
saw the grime and poverty of the characters' lives. The style
was more realistic, less romanticized, than what had gone
before – we saw bare, dirty feet rather than the picturesque
pampooties that were worn even in the original Abbey
production. Yet it was also wilder, stranger and more plugged
into the anarchic, carnivalesque comedy of Synge's
imagination. There was a soft, tender yearning and a frantic,
compulsive energy. The playing was precisely detailed, with
each moment full of deliberation and control, yet it also
unleashed all the gothic and grotesque elements of the writing.
The characters were rooted and credible, but they also
expanded into physical caricatures of themselves.

In that 1982 *Playboy*, the actors seemed to inhabit the same
stage but come from different planets. Brid Brennan's Pegeen
was still, watchful and, for all her outbursts of bossy rage,
intensely innocent. Marie Mullen's Widow Quin, by contrast,
was nonchalant, impervious, avid for a man but too worldly to
be hurt, her eyes hungry, predatory but also full of salty
humour. Mick Lally's Old Mahon was a hulking bear, Ray
McBride's Michael James an evasive ferret. Maeliosa Stafford's
Christy expanded and strutted as Sean McGinley's Shawn
Keogh shrank and lurked. And all this human variety created a

shifting, unpredictable universe in which no simple chain of events could be traced from cause to effect. In the constant interplay of contrary moods and conflicting impulses, words were not just static poetry but gestures of continual self-invention. The language had restored to it the theatrical energy of people making themselves up through speech. The old question – how do I know what I think until I see what I say? – hovered over every line. Synge's own paradoxical phrase for the kind of national mood that enables great art – 'provisionally permanent' – came to mind, capturing perfectly the fusion of a permanent text with a radically contingent performance that is the essence of theatre.

Just as the 1982 *Playboy* drew on apparently unrelated productions like *Island Protected By a Bridge of Glass*, so it was continued in productions of other plays, most immediately the superb 1983 production of M.J. Molloy's *The Wood of the Whispering*, again directed by Garry Hynes and again featuring Mick Lally, Sean McGinley, Maeliosa Stafford, Ray McBride and Marie Mullen, and the breathtaking 1985 premiere of Tom Murphy's *Bailegangaire*, with Mullen, Mary McEvoy and Siobhán McKenna. Each, of course, had its own dynamic, but each, too, reminded us that Druid's Synge is not just about Synge. *Bailegangaire* is a wonderfully original masterpiece in its own right, yet the resonance of *The Playboy* could be felt in two ways. One, most obviously, was the language of Mommo's story, a Gaelicized English that represented the fullest linguistic flowering in contemporary theatre of seeds that Synge had planted. The other was the absolute confidence with which that production approached the unusual structure of the play, in which the world of Mommo's baroque narrative co-exists on stage with the more mundane reality of the contemporary action. It is hardly accidental that the split is, again, that between a gallous story and some dirty deeds, or that the brilliance of the production was rooted in Hynes's evolution, through *The Playboy*, of a theatrical style precisely calibrated to just such a conflict between what we see and what we hear.

If Druid's Synge is about more than Synge, however, it has always seemed to me that it is also about another, curiously absent figure – Samuel Beckett. On the surface, this may seem a ridiculous suggestion. Beckett was an early presence in Druid's repertoire: the company presented *Act Without Words II* in its very first season in the summer of 1975, and *Happy Days* the following year. But there have been just two Beckett productions since: *Endgame* in 1981 and *Waiting for Godot* in 1987. Yet it could be argued that there is so little of Beckett in Hynes's repertoire for the same reason that there are, allegedly, no camels mentioned in the Koran: his is such a constant presence that there is no need to advertise it.

This reticence, however, obscures something very significant. One of Garry Hynes's great achievements has been, as it were, to reunite the two great theatrical scions of the Dublin Protestant professional class: Synge and Beckett. This process took hold in that production of *The Wood of the Whispering*, which imagined the play almost as if it were a collaboration between Synge and Beckett, the former's lush, highly charged language spoken by the latter's homeless, tragi-comic denizens of a fractured and indifferent universe. Beckett, in a sense, was drawn into Druid's continuing quarrel with the romantic official notion of the 'beautiful and tradition-rich places of the West', an argument that has shaped the company's history from its earliest days right up to and including its staging of Martin McDonagh's *Leenane Trilogy*. The vision of an unromantic *Playboy*, with its demythologized West was carried through into *The Wood of the Whispering*, where the West was imagined as a broken, Beckettian world. It is not accidental that the epigraph in the programme for *The Wood* was taken from Beckett's sardonic puncturing of urban nostalgia for a rustic utopia in his novel Murphy:

> Oh hand in hand, let us return to the land of our birth, the bogs, the moors, the glens, the lakes, the rivers, the streams, the brooks, the mists, the – er – fens, the – er – glens, by tonight's mail-train.

This exposure of an underlying empathy between Synge and Beckett is rooted, paradoxically, in the perception of a different kind of cultural continuity to that evoked by Charles Haughey:

a continuity of outsiders. It picks up on one of the angularities of Irish twentieth-century theatre history – the deep feeling that, in a culture that was inventing a settled homeland, the real place for the artist to be was with the homeless, the unsettled, the nomadic.

The affinity between Synge and Beckett that has been illuminated by Druid is a matter both of form and content. Beckett's mode is all about the gap between story and deed, between words and action – the very disjunction that Garry Hynes has explored in her Synge productions. Think of Winnie in *Happy Days*, sending out a stream of language to reassure herself that she is leading a normal existence while we can see that she is buried up to her neck in the ground. Or of the last lines of *Waiting for Godot*, with their simple distillation of the conflict between what the actors say and what they do:

> **Estragon:** Well? Shall we go?
> **Vladimir:** Yes, let's go.
> *They do not move.*

But there is an affinity of content, too, that is rooted in the early history of the Irish theatre movement. When Shawn Keogh remarks on Pegeen 'picking a dirty tramp up from the highways of the world', the image now reminds us of Estragon and Vladimir, and of Beckett's vision of humanity itself as a dirty tramp on the highways of a careless world. And there is here a chain of tradition. Some of the very first stirrings of the Irish national theatre movement from which Synge emerged used very similar images and settings. P.T. McGinley's one-act play *Eilís agus an Bhean Dhéirce,* presented in Dublin by The Daughters of Erin in 1901, and Douglas Hyde's *An Tincéar agus an tSidheóg,* presented the following year, were crucial forerunners of the Abbey. Both dealt with what were then called 'tinkers', and both ended with a 'tinker' departing the stage with a fierce curse on settled humanity. The image entered the Abbey tradition through the collaboration of Hyde with W.B. Yeats and Lady Gregory in the 1902 play *Where There is Nothing.* This play again attempted to imagine the Traveller way of life as a rebellion against bourgeois smugness, and, indirectly, against the niceties of a respectable Protestant upbringing. The play tells the story of Paul Rutledge, a landlord, who decides to become a Traveller. John Synge, of course, became Paul Rutledge, tramping the hills and valleys of Wicklow. And he turned the rather gauche wish-fulfilment of these early plays into vibrant art in *The Shadow of the Glen*, *The Tinker's Wedding* and *The Well of the Saints*. Those last two plays, in turn, helped to shape Beckett's imagination, peopled as it is by wanderers, nomads and homeless refugees from a normality that has ceased to exist.

If all of this seems no more than an abstract historical connection, it has been given flesh in Garry Hynes's fusion of Beckett and Synge. It is, indeed, embodied in a series of performances by Marie Mullen that runs from the Widow Quin, a woman alone, in *The Playboy* in 1982, to the starkly Beckettian interpretation of Sadie Tubridy in *The Wood of the Whispering* and back to a Synge filtered through Beckett with her Mary Byrne in *The Tinker's Wedding* and Mary Doul in *The Well of the Saints* in 2004 and 2005. Bold, mischievous, at ease with the flow of words and the stillness of silence, these performances form a living bridge between the contrary elements of Synge's imagination, the symbolic minimalism that heavily influenced Beckett and the salty mediaeval lustiness that makes Synge's texts so vividly alive. Mullen's apparent agelessness (there is almost thirty years between her second coming as Mary Byrne and her first performance of the role in 1976) has given her access to a sense of what is genuinely timeless in Synge – not a vapid flight from history, but an ability to create images and archetypes that transcend it. She has incarnated a Synge at once imperturbably ancient and forever full of youthful vibrancy and cheek. And in doing so she summed up the point of Druid's Synge: that theatre can do more than one thing at any one time.

Illustration 3: Islanders on Inishere.
Synge Photo 46 (TCD)

3 | Shift
Hugo Hamilton

The first thing we noticed going out to Aran was the light. It was coming from the opposite direction and felt strange. To a person brought up in Dublin, on the east coast of Ireland, the world seems to be turned around a full hundred and eighty degrees when you take the boat from Galway out to the Islands. The white glimmer of sunlight that you expect to see when coming ashore is right there ahead of you on the way out to sea. The feeling of leaving becomes confused with the feeling of going home. It's like an inverse homecoming, something that must be similar to getting on the plane in autumn and landing somewhere on the far side of the world in spring. On the Naomh Eanna ferry out to Irishmore, it felt as though we were going backwards in time, travelling into the mirror. We were staring into the light over the Atlantic. We could barely see the shape of the three Islands in the distance. We could smell the sea and the diesel fumes and feel the throb of the engines in everything we touched. We could hear the murmur of Irish being spoken around us on the boat and became aware, without saying it openly, that we were no longer facing east, towards London, towards the buzz of Europe, but west, into an older, untouched world.

> In my cottage I have never heard a word of English from the women except when they were speaking to the pigs or to the dogs ...

A small group of us had come from Dublin after school in
the summer to spend some time on the island, to see this
remote place with our own eyes before it disappeared. People
were talking about Aran as if it was the last part of Ireland that
was left intact. The country was moving on. Yoghurt had just
been discovered. Men wore beards and moustaches.
Everything was going electric. New music, new cars, new
fashions from London and Paris. A photographer in one of the
daily newspapers had captured the change that was taking place
in the country that summer in a front page shot of a slender
young woman dressed in a white mini-skirt, high white boots
and a broad-rimmed white hat, lifting her suitcase onto the
train at Euston Station with a nun in a brown habit waiting in
line behind her.

We travelled west to the Aran Islands with one eye on the
future and the other on the past. As we arrived on the pier in
Kilronan, the afternoon sun was shining away towards the
mainland. We walked up towards the American Bar which
seemed to have taken on the function of the island waiting
room, where people looked out to see if the boat was coming
in, where men spoke about the weather and decided whether
the boat would go back out again or whether you might be
trapped on the island for another night. The people leaving the
island were heading down towards the pier and the people
arriving were filling their places at the American Bar. Some of
the tourists were already heading out along the road to see the
promontory fort at Dun Aengus, on foot, in cars, on pony and
traps, on rented bicycles. We were staying on the other side of
the island at Killeanny, so we made our way past the dance hall,
past the low cliffs with the ivy, out along the road towards the
small fishing harbour and the white strand which they call *'tra
na ladies'* or the ladies beach.

> The day was unbearably sultry, and the sand and sea near us
> were crowded with half-naked women …

As we began to explore the island, we took notice of the
strange, empty landscape around us. We saw the small Aran
fields and the high stone walls, made with sharp grey limestone

rocks. We noticed how the tarred road was always fringed with a line of white sand and grass. We smelled the turf smoke and heard the sound of enamel buckets as we passed by the houses. Here and there a dog accompanied us part of the way and we understood how little traffic there was on this road and what a novelty we must have been, the strangers from Dublin. We saw the airstrip in the distance with a single red fire engine parked in the middle and around twenty-five island donkeys roaming freely on the grass. We were told that every one of them had an owner, but they had the freedom of the island to come and go as they pleased, laughing at everyone as they went. We went out to the Glasen rocks and the cliffs facing into the Atlantic, and saw nobody out there. We saw balls of foam floating in from the sea and heard the booming sound of the waves smashing across the terraced rocks and into hollow caves underneath us.

> There has been a storm for the last twenty-four hours, and I have been wandering the cliffs till my hair is stiff with salt. Immense masses of spray were flying up from the base of the cliff, and were caught at times by the wind and whirled away to fall at some distance from the shore. When one of these happened to fall on me, I had to crouch down for an instant, wrapped and blinded in a white hail of foam.

We felt the jagged shapes through our light running shoes. We were used to pavements and maybe to the more rounded granite shapes on the east coast, so it took a while to get used to walking across limestone blades that were sometimes sticking up vertically. In other places, the cliffs were like a flat stage with large cracks running through them and the occasional white granite rock left over from the ice age, called the Aran visitors.

> … here I realized that toes have a natural use, for I found myself jumping towards any tiny crevice in the rock before me, and clinging with an eager grip in which all the muscles of my feet ached from the exertion.

On the way back from the cliffs, we saw the men working in the fields. Sometimes we saw women or children walking along the road and we noticed that they took the side of the road, close to the wall, while we generally walked in the middle. Mostly we saw nobody at all and it was only after some days that we understood how far away and how empty this landscape really was, how hard it must be to live here, away from the mainland, away from the reassurance of shops and crowded streets. At night, it was so dark that you could see the stars very clearly, not only the main shapes like the plough, but a whole lacy spray of white in between. It was so dark sometimes that we had to hold our arms out in front of us and grope at the stone walls to make sure we were still on the road.

> ... no light anywhere except the phosphorescence of the sea, and an occasional rift in the clouds that showed the stars behind them.

In Tigh Fitz bar in Killeanny, we heard the men speaking in Irish and telling great stories that sometimes ran on indefinitely until they ended with a sudden punctuation; that's my story. We heard the story of how a plane once landed on the island during the First World War and how the cows and horses were all frightened because they were not used to the sound of engines and motorbikes. There was one horse driven mad for weeks, running crazy all over the island, day and night, with all the islanders trying to trap him and bring him back to his senses. When a young man with a rope tied around his waist finally sneaked up to harness the horse in a moment of exhaustion one day, he went fully out of his mind and ran out into the waves on the beach at '*tra na ladies*', taking the young man with him. We heard other stories of drowning and stories of the supernatural. We heard the story of the Hollywood director who once came to Aran and found a brother and sister who were so handsome that he asked them to go back with him and spend the rest of their lives in the movies in America. When they were going away on the boat, waving at the people they were leaving behind on the pier at Kilronan, the brother suddenly changed his mind and jumped off to swim ashore again, while the sister stayed on board and went to America where she became a famous actress and they never laid eyes on each other again.

They say on the island that he can tell as many lies as four men.

Of course, we had studied *The Playboy of the Western World* at school, so we knew that a man would invent any story around himself in order to attract the admiration of a woman. Not only that, it meant a man would fabricate his own biography in order to get shelter and belonging, that he would turn himself into anything and fit himself into any image required of him in order to be accepted. We knew that the inspiration for the play came from a story of a man who said he had killed his own father with a blow of a spade and was hidden by the islanders in a hole on the island while the police were searching for him. We knew that the word 'shift' had caused a riot when the play was performed first in the Abbey Theatre. It was the word used long ago for a woman's undergarments, but had already fallen out of use by then, so the offence taken from it by the audience was belated and antiquarian. We knew that the prudish, nationalist inspiration which sparked this riot had angered Yeats and provoked his famous line '... you have disgraced yourselves,' a phrase which we often used against each other in class with condescending genius. We were also aware in the meantime, that the word 'shift' had evolved or been recast once more with an entirely different meaning. In a devout, Catholic Ireland of closet heterosexuals, shift now took on the meaning of getting off with, scoring, or generally being successful with a woman. We never used the word ourselves because it was a country term, which came from the dancehall culture, where shifting a woman meant getting her from the inside to the outside. Either that or it came from the new car culture of changing gears to a higher speed. But we knew it meant much more and implied end results that went far beyond that, something that involved making up any amount of lies and stories to attract the admiration of a woman. We also knew that the verb 'breagadh' in the Irish language had multiple meaning, telling lies as well as courting, shifting, or flirting.

> The women and girls, when they had no men with them, usually tried to make fun with me …

> 'Here is my little sister, stranger, who will give you her arm.'

> And so it went on. Quiet as these women are on ordinary occasions, when two or three of them are gathered together in their holiday petticoats and shawls, they are as wild and capricious as the women who live in towns.

We got talking to some of the Aran girls at the dancehall. The girls from Killeanny kept accusing us of trying to grow beards to pretend that we were men. They said they had seen more hair on the back of a door. They asked if they could touch our faces and then described it with an Irish word 'meigeal', at which they all started grinning and looking into our eyes. The more they said the word, the more they laughed outright. 'Meigeal' is the Irish word for a goat's beard, but it also has multiple meaning which we could not guess at the time.

> The women of this island are before conventionality, and share some of the liberal features that are thought peculiar to the women of Paris and New York.

> The direct sexual instincts are not weak on the island, but they are so subordinated to the instincts of the family that they rarely lead to irregularity.

We met the girls from Killeanny frequently along the road or outside their houses, but rarely in the pub. Even when we asked them to come for a drink, it was only early on in the evening that they would come with us, because late at night, the bar was mostly taken over by men and tourists. Instead, they invited us into their houses for tea and scones that they had made, sitting us down at the table to watch us eating, but never eating themselves in our company.

> The complete absence of shyness or self-consciousness in most of these people gives them a peculiar charm, and when this young and beautiful woman leaned across my knees to look nearer at some photographs that pleased her, I felt more than ever the strange simplicity of the island life.

In Tigh Fitz, the old men would sometimes ask us if we had any girlfriends. When time moved on, they would start singing. 'The Rocks a Bawn' was like a hit single on the island and somebody had to sing it every night or nobody could go home. And the singer often needed to hold the hand of another living person while they sang, usually that of a stranger, winding it around like a barrel organ to keep the song coming.

> … do you never be thinking on the young girls? The time I was a young man, the divil a one of them could I look on without wishing to marry her.

One night in Tigh Fitz, one of our lads from Dublin got talking to a young Dutch woman who was staying on the island for the summer. She had been in an accident and was recovering with a plaster around her leg, sitting on the bench with the leg stretched out and the painted toes sticking out the other end, while an old man wound her hand around and around in circles. She was so beautiful that everyone was blind to her injuries. They all wanted to talk to her and tell her any amount of lies. They told jokes and stories, and maybe it was inevitable that it was one of our lads from Dublin, the most handsome among us, the one with the deepest beard and the best stories of all, who finally put his arm around her and helped with her crutches to make sure she didn't fall over when she was leaving.

The following day, we all went walking up to an ancient church above Killeanny village. We climbed the hill beyond the cottages with the Dutch girl and her new chaperone following some distance behind us. She was wearing a red tartan skirt that afternoon, which flapped in the wind every now and again, making life on crutches even more difficult. At the monastic ruin of Teampaill Bheannain, the breeze frequently revealed the entire stump of plaster. We read the historical information on the sign and looked at the crumbling walls covered in yellow lichen. Occasionally, we understood for a brief moment how ancient this place was, but we were always brought back to the present by the sound of the crutches and sight of the tartan in the wind.

On the way back through Killeanny that afternoon, we
came walking by the cottages and saw hundreds of salted fish
laid out along the walls to dry like small white dish-cloths. Each
one of the cottages had fishing implements outside, lobster
pots, oars, and buoys. At the harbour, we saw the tide gone out
and the black seaweed draped along the rocks. Some men and
dogs were sitting on the small pier.

We carried on walking past the cottages with the Dutch girl
and her chaperone out in front of us this time. The crutches
were clicking slowly along the road with no hurry, making it
sound like a hospital ward in the open air. Now and again she
stopped to take the weight off her hands, hopping around for a
moment on her good leg and falling into her chaperone with
her arms around him. At one of the cottages there was an old
woman leaning at the gate, looking out at the sea and watching
the slow procession coming towards her. She began to talk to
us, first of all saying it was a fine day to be walking and doing
nothing. She wanted to know where the girl was from and
what happened to her leg. We explained that she had broken
her leg in a car accident on the mainland and that she was
spending the summer on the island until it was healed. The old
woman began to laugh, saying there was not much to do on the
island for a woman with a plaster on her leg.

> … they crowded round me and began jeering and shrieking at
> me because I am not married. A dozen screamed at a time, and
> so rapidly that I could not understand all they were saying, yet I
> was able to make out that they were taking advantage of the
> absence of their husbands to give me the full volume of their
> contempt. Some little boys who were listening threw
> themselves down, writhing with laughter among the seaweed,
> and the young girls grew red with embarrassment and stared
> down into the surf.

By now the Dutch girl and her partner had already begun to
move ahead along the road, while we were still listening to the
old woman and answering her provocative questions with
shrugs and smiles. She asked us why we had no girlfriends and
what was wrong with all the island girls walking up and down
the road day and night with no crutches.

> Their skirts do not come much below the knee, and show their
> powerful legs …

The old woman smiled. She was looking at us with a humorous idleness, leaning lazily with her elbow on the wall. We could see the ancient teeth left over in her mouth and the deep lines across her face. We could see the marks of the weather and the wind and the rain around her sunken cheeks, but underneath, she had the expression of a young Killeanny girl. Nothing could hide the mischievous optimism in her eyes as she watched us drifting away and called out a final exhortation in Irish behind us. '*Scaoil amach an deabhaillín,*' she said with a wink (Let out the little divileen).

We had been misinformed by the landscape, by the wind, by the desolate features of this island. Now we began to understand why we felt the world had been turned around for us. It was not just the direction of the sunlight. It was all the things we had expected to come from London, from Europe and New York. They were here on the Aran Islands in plenty. Let out the little divileen.

> … I would be right to marry a girl out of this island, for there
> were nice women in it, fine fat girls, who would be strong, and
> have plenty of children, and not be wasting my money on me.

Excerpts from *The Aran Islands* by John Millington Synge.

Illustration 4: Portrait of J. M. Synge. TCD MS 4367/1

4 | A Glass of Champagne
Marina Carr

Chekhov stands beside a huge blue door. He waits expectantly. Fixes his tie. Clears his throat. The door slides open onto an immense black sky strippled with stars. Enter John Millington Synge, dishevelled, confused.

Chekhov: Welcome.

Synge: Where am I?

Chekhov: I'll explain that in due course. How was the journey?

Synge: What journey? Last I remember I was lying in my hospital bed. A red-haired nurse ... why are they always red-haired? ... crooning in my ear. 'It's all right', she whispers. 'It's far from all right', I whisper back. And next thing I'm watching myself die.

Chekhov: One of the great experiences life has to offer.

Synge: I looked so small, like a swaddled baby arrayed for a christening. Why would anyone want to kill such a puny harmless thing? That's what I was thinking. And then the swirling dust, the frightening cold, the chortling vacuum ... and here.

Looks around.

Is that the Earth?

Chekhov: I believe so ... and there's the moon.

Synge: Different from the astronomy books.

Chekhov: Yes. Very. Allow me to introduce myself. Anton Pavlovich Chekhov.

Holds out his hand.

Synge: John Millington Synge.

Chekhov: They sent me ahead of the welcoming party. You're my first so excuse me if I'm a little nervous.

Synge: Your first.

Chekhov: Yes. The others will be here shortly. They sent me ahead as they said we'd have things in common.

Synge: Like What?

Chekhov: Well breathing difficulties, early death, the theatre. That sort of thing.

Synge: You write for the theatre?

Chekhov: Yes. I do. I did.

Synge: Any good?

Chekhov: The odd line here and there. Not really. No.

Synge: Me either.

Chekhov: But I love it. I loved it.

Synge: The theatre. Yes. Put me in a darkened room, bright up the lights and I swear to god I'd watch anything.

Chekhov: Well we put on a lot of plays here. Some promising young ones coming up. They'll be sent down shortly of course.

Synge: Sent down?

Chekhov: Down into the world, the living steaming world. The lucky things.

Synge: And us?

Chekhov: We've had our turn. Most don't get one. Most are passed over. At least we got a crack at it.

Synge: I'm only thirty-seven.

Chekhov: I know. I was forty-four.

Synge: And what took you out?

Chekhov: The lungs. The women. A woman. The writing magic flown. The time allotted gone.

Synge: You got longer than me.

Chekhov: It's not a competition.

Synge: Isn't it. Somehow I've always believed that I'd be left alive as long as I observed certain laws.

Chekhov: Very old testament.

Synge: Yes my mother was a religious nut ... but what those laws are I could never figure out.

Chekhov: It is no shame to die young. But I know what you mean. I spent the first couple of years here apologizing to everyone for dying. They don't care. They really don't. If I may offer you a little advice, John. May I call you John?

Synge: Yes.

Chekhov: Eternity cares nothing for the private sorrows of us brave little earthlings.

Synge: Then I care nothing for eternity.

Chekhov: You're in shock. Say nothing for a while, just watch and wait. Trust me. Don't be afraid. Can I offer you a glass of champagne?

Synge: I had champagne last evening with my nephew.

Chekhov: All the best people have champagne on their death beds.

Synge: Did you?

Chekhov: I was force fed it by a German doctor and when I died the cork flew out of the bottle. My biographers have made much of this detail. Really I was just trying to get another glass to bolster me for the gallop here.

He opens the champagne and pours two glasses, hands one to Synge.

Synge: Thank you.

Chekhov: A ghost cigar.

Synge: Why not.

They light them and puff out clouds of silver smoke.

Chekhov: Smoking is a pleasure I'm re-discovering. I had to give it up when I was alive.

Synge: Is my mother here?

Chekhov: Your mother.

Synge: Yes. She died last year.

Chekhov: Then she must be around somewhere.

Synge: They didn't brief you on my mother..

Chekhov: They didn't mention her.

Synge: No doubt she'll be thrilled to hear I didn't survive a year without her … so who is this advance party coming to meet me?

Chekhov: Poets, painters, playwrights, philosophers, a few dancers and a horde of bawdy actors.

Synge: I love actors.

Chekhov: I prefer actresses.

Synge: I suppose that's what I meant. Will Shakespeare be coming?

Chekhov: Everyone wants to be met by him.

Synge: Have you met him?

Chekhov: Oh yes. You'd want to see what he's writing now. He's going before the committee again soon.

Synge: What committee?

Chekhov: The selection committee ... that's what they're called though no one has ever seen them. He wants to go back ... we all do.

Synge: And will they let him?

Chekhov: He came close last time ... too soon it was said.

Synge: Too soon? Then what chance do I have?

Chekhov: I ask myself the same.

Synge: What's he like?

Chekhov: He has one golden wing. He fishes all the time.

Synge: Is he any good?

Chekhov: What do you think?

Synge: I'd be surprised if he was a good fisherman unless he chants some witchery to draw them in. Too good a writer to be much use for anything else if you ask me. I've met plenty of fishermen. Like everything else it's an art form. Fishing. Takes a lifetime to perfect.

Chekhov: He disappears for days, years, whatever time is called here. He goes off fishing with his son. The young Hamnet.

Synge: Is he still eleven?

Chekhov: That child was never eleven. You'll meet them. He goes everywhere with the boy.

Synge: Do you ... did you have children?

Chekhov: No

Synge: No. Me either. Does that matter in the grand scheme of things?

Chekhov: I don't know about the grand scheme but it matters to me.

Synge: I thought I had abundance of time. I was just beginning to figure what it's all about and bam, it's over. Last night I was drinking champagne with Edward. We talked about birds. Birds. This time of year I like to be in the hills or out on the Islands but I was having surgery, I thought I'd go mad cooped up and my nephew came with champagne and he spoke to me about birds and it was ordinary, I was even a bit bored, but my God from here it was glorious. And then he left and I went to bed. And that's it. Is this a dream? Will I wake in the morning and laugh that I took you for real?

Chekhov: Oh I'm real. Real as only a shade can be. Another drop?

Synge: This champagne is good. Well if this is eternity it is not as cold as I thought it would be. It's light, it bubbles, it sparkles.

Chekhov: It has its ethers too. Its sulphour and vapours, its whirling terrors and its night sweats but you'll meet those soon enough.

Synge: And the creator? Do I get an audience with him?

Chekhov: If you do you'll be the first.

Synge: He's not here.

Chekhov: There are ruins of old palaces rumoured to be his. Moulds of rubbled turquoise and some rock no one can identify. No one is sure who lived there. He hasn't been here in a while. If ever.

Synge: Then what's the point of prolonging it if he's not here?

Chekhov: You don't have to.

Synge: I can die again.

Chekhov: Most opt to finish it in the clay.

Synge: They don't go for this?

Chekhov: This is nothing. It's not like this. This suit of clothes I wear is not a suit of clothes. I am a different creature away from here. You'll see. You'll be given the choice. Don't be afraid. I tell myself that forty times a minute. Don't be afraid. Just look on it as one of those revenge tragedies.

Synge: Who revenges who?

Chekhov: It is nothing like you have ever experienced.

Synge: So these are not champagne glasses and this is not a cigar and that backdrop is not the distant earth.

Chekhov: And you are not John Millington Synge.

Synge: Then who am I?

Chekhov: Some ancient thing that suffers and desires. I'm a novice here too. They swirl through the air John. You will swirl through the air all beak and talons. The light is different here, not for the faint hearted. There will be times you will weep for the quiet of dust.

Synge: Well I know one thing now.

Chekhov: And what is that?

Synge: This is what I should've been writing about. Eternity. I didn't trust it enough. Wasted more paper writing about girleens in shebeens and little mammy's boys who wouldn't know one end of a woman from the other. You know I did twelve drafts of a play once. It got worse and worse with each draft.

Chekhov: What was it about?

Synge: Aah … nonsense about a playboy who wasn't. Where I come from no one had sex. Or if they did it was by accident. That's what I was trying to write about but big corseted mammy Ireland was having none of it. Out on the Island they were different. Savages. The women were savages. They attacked me one day on the pier. I was the only man on the Island. They were high from watching husbands, fathers, brothers, sons, loading cattle onto boats for the fair. And then suddenly the men all gone and me alone with seventy, ninety, a hundred women on the pier, all shrieking at me, 'Why aren't you married? Come on show us why you're not married.'– and pulling and tearing at my clothes.

Chekhov: I love Islands.

Synge: And the women used to stand in the sea to bath themselves. Women to drive you mad. Not their fault, they're just washing themselves in the sea, it's what they've always done, but still, from the cliffs, something to behold. And then sometimes the men would take me out with them in the currach. They were different out there on the open sea. I was different. Our mood would accord itself with wonderful fineness to the suggestions of the day and the ancient gaelic we spoke was of such divine simplicity that I would have liked to turn the prow to the west and row with them forever. But all of that is over.

Chekhov: Yes. All gone.

Synge: Chekhov you said your name was.

Chekhov: That's right.

Synge: I read a story of yours in some French journal a couple of years back … about a little boy travelling through the Steppe with a priest and his uncle … that was yours.

Chekhov: You read it?

Synge: Yes. And what's more I loved it. The boy … was that you?

Chekhov: When I was nine or ten my mother decided to go in search of her father's grave. So she hired horses and a cart and we all piled on. My father stayed at home to our great delight. Me, Sasha, Kolya, Masha, the babies and my mother heading off on an adventure. We rode for a month through the mountains, sleeping under the stars, cooking by campfire, washing in streams.

Synge: And did you find your grandfather's grave?

Chekhov: No we never did I wonder is she still alive … and Olga … Masha … you wouldn't know would you?

Synge: I'm sorry.

Chekhov: Pointless even asking.

Synge: Who are Olga and Masha?

Chekhov: Olga was my wife. Masha? Who was Masha? My sister I suppose, but more than that. It would be good to see those three women again. Olga was an actress with the Moscow Arts. Faithless, light headed but a lifeline to me. I hardly saw her. And Masha … poor old Masha … my work horse. It goes without saying they hated one another. And my wise old mother in the middle of them, reading her bible. I never said goodbye. Always in flight. I thought if I kept on the move I'd somehow beat this disease. I never dreamt it would happen so quickly. I'm a doctor. I've seen plenty of death but I could never apply it to myself. To be snuffed out like that. That was for others. And to be landed here. Irony of ironies. The sceptic in eternity. I still don't believe in it but here I am. Here you are. And I'm rattling on about myself and I said I wouldn't. I have no manners it seems.

Synge: Your manners are fine.

Chekhov: Well the champagne is finished. Will I open another bottle or do you feel up to the maelstrom?

Synge: Couldn't we just sit here for ever and drink and smoke cigars? If there was a violin around I'd play for you. That's all I ever wanted to do, play the violin …

Chekhov: We can send for a violin.

Synge: Then do. I'll open another bottle. Let's have a wake.

Chekhov: You mean mourn our own passing. I'm all for that. All right, you serenade me and I'll sing you all the Russian hymns my father taught me.

The blue door slides open. Shakespeare stands there with his son Hamnet.

Shakespeare: Where's this poet fiddler? Champagne! Fantastic! Will Shakespeare. This is Hamnet, my son. It is such a pleasure to finally meet the man who wrote *Riders to the Sea.*

Better than the Greeks. Now tell me all the news from the old country. Play Hamnet, play little man, I always like music as the lamps go out.

And fade on the scene as Hamnet plays on the violin.

End

Illustration 5: Synge's Paris: The playwright's room in the Hotel Corneille. TCD MS 4367/7

5 | A White Horse on the Street: Remembering Synge in Paris

Vincent Woods

February 10:

The Café des Arts after a poetry reading. A slightly drunken German woman in our company tries to explain the significance of the pattern on the Aran jumper. She strokes the white synthetic stitches on my friend's chest. He already knows all about the tradition: has read *Riders To The Sea* in French and English but is too polite to tell her. This chill night he's probably wearing the jumper more for warmth than any nostalgia for Ireland. 'Each family had their own particular stitch, yes? So if you were drowned and the body was washed up they'd know it was you.' She pokes him with a determined finger. 'I could repair this jumper for you. On the Islands they'd make you an exact copy, and it would be yours - unique - nothing much has changed, you know, since Synge was there.'

February 12:

An Englishman at a party tells me he remembers seeing Beckett walking in the Jardins de Luxembourg. 'Always impeccably dressed', he says. 'I was amazed; these beautiful Italian suits, really expensive, perfectly cut. I don't know what I expected from reading him, some kind of tramp, I suppose. More Irish.' Maybe he didn't mean it like that.

February 17:

A young Arab man, beautiful, quick-smiled, in an expensive-looking Aran jumper argues with a policeman about his motorbike – tax maybe, or parking. It's snowing slightly, white flakes on black hair. You'd know him again if his body came washing in on the tide. The policeman gives up, shrugs, ignores the small audience, steps hard on the pedals of his own bike, and away. A lovely girl steps out of Café Ness carrying the trophy leather jacket. She kisses her hero, they laugh, heads thrown back to catch snow in their mouths. Then she gets on behind him and they zoom off, giddy, vivid, the lights of the Eiffel Tower spangling the night sky.

February 23:

In a small restaurant on Rue du Pot de Fer I look around and notice five people wearing Aran knits. One chunky polo-neck; one handsome, worn, off-white jersey with what looks like another green one underneath; a waistcoat and two cardigans. All at different tables. American, Chinese and French. Maybe they're expecting really bad floods, maybe they know something I don't know. If the drunken woman were here she'd have a great time.

February 27:

I'm thinking about a moment from years ago, a moment that reminds me of the cruel truthfulness at the heart of *Playboy*. It's in a pub in Leitrim. A publican stares entranced at the wildlife programme on the telly over the bar. A cheetah is chasing a gazelle. 'Look at it, look at the speed of him, the power.' Her eyes sparkle with excitement. 'He'll catch her yet, he'll bring her down - look at that.' The cheetah downs the exhausted prey and mauls it. 'That's the stuff! That's the end of hunger for him.' She turns away reluctantly to fill a pint, glancing back to see what's on next. She has the loveliest laugh you might ever hear – gay and light and without a care in the world. It reminds me so much of Pegeen's line about the hanged dog and the licence and the peeler. The casual cruelty, the jubilant tilt of the head, the lilt of the language.

You'd wonder what became of Pegeen after the Playboy went east. Did she give in and marry Shaneen Keogh? Or become a committed spinster, running the business with a bitter grip when Michael James shambled to the grave? Maybe she went to America, lived to be ninety, came back to Mayo a loud Yank like Gar's aunt in *Philadelphia Here I Come*. Saw the first man on the moon and JFK. Boasted about her youthful fame in a hothouse Rest Home on the Upper West Side. 'You never lost it, Peggy, you musta kissed that Blarney Stone.' Shambling on her zimmer frame. Maybe she drowned on the Titanic.

Or survived.

March 1:

Sending the almost-final draft of Deirdre (*A Cry From Heaven*) to Jocelyn Clarke at the Abbey. Despite cuts it's four pages longer. But then there's the new long speech for Ness at the end and a longer one for Conor. I think it's stronger – tighter, leaner; I've got rid of words, phrases, lines that seemed wrong or hokumy. 'And the snow begins' is gone – Olivier, who is to direct, will be delighted …

***

A friend here says to me:
'It's a really brave thing to make a new Deirdre, really gutsy.'
'Or mad,' I think to myself.
'And know what?' she says 'one thing your Deirdre must have – she must have balls!'

March 3:

Bitterly cold here: the fountain in the Place de l'Estrapade is frozen solid, shattered stalactites of water caught in mid-air. The cast-metal cherub faces gleam out from behind thin masks of ice, made more beautiful, somehow, by the transparent sheen. Someone said it was minus thirteen degrees last night;

not sure I believe that – but you wonder how the homeless survive sleeping out on the street corners around here. I'm reminded of a night in autumn (I think September) 1995 when I noticed a homeless couple asleep in the arches at the side of the Odéon. The Abbey's great production of *The Well of the Saints* had just opened and I was leaving the theatre late. I stopped to watch the man and woman wrapped tight in their sleeping bags, rough faces in a kind of alert slumber. There was a crutch on the ground between them. I put money into each sleeping bag and watched them for another while. I was going south the next day and I thought about Martin and Mary Doul and their journey south across 'a power of deep rivers with floods in them … ' I was glad to be heading towards the sun instead, and I liked to imagine this pair waking to find the unexpected money, picking up sticks and shuffling off into the dawn. Probably cursing whoever had given them so little.

March 5:

I wonder about Yeats's famous exhortation to Synge to go back to Ireland and go to the Aran Islands etc. To be taken with a slight pinch of salt, I'd say. Like these few anecdotes that come back out of nowhere in particular: in 1997 or '98 a man on a minibus near Foxford assured me that Yeats had had an affair with F.R. Higgins. 'They were definitely lovers,' he said, 'a teacher of mine told me for a fact.'

Then there was the story I heard about a musician, now dead, who claimed the great poet had made a pass at him – on the top of Ben Bulben! And the yarn about the local man, well sozzled, who wandered into a session of the Yeats Summer School in Drumcliffe about thirty years ago. The academics are considering the meaning of the famous epitaph, and yer man sways onto his feet. 'Cast a cold eye,' he slurs, 'on life on death.' He pauses for dramatic effect, looks around the room. Spits it out: 'And the horse goes clippetty fucking clop!'

March 7:

Looking over earlier notes on why I wanted to write a new *Deirdre*: all the themes here: love, sex, power, jealousy, conflict, violence, death. Easy to see why Yeats and Synge were drawn to the story – it doesn't come much more primal. It's still a challenge to make life of it all, to make 'the saga people' live and breathe and love and fuck.

And more formally: I was fascinated by Deirdre long before I knew that anyone at all had written a play about her: as a child of eight or nine I first read the story in an old schoolbook and was drawn to it again and again, compelled by something I didn't understand but felt instinctively. There was something raw, shocking and deeply moving in the simplicity of the story and in the red and black illustrations. I could imagine the blood of the slaughtered calf on the snow; I could imagine the ferocity of the battle that raged outside while Deirdre and Naoise played chess inside; I somehow knew that love and death and some other magnetic force between people were all mixed up here, mixed into a power that stirred and disturbed me.

Returning to the Deirdre theme as an adult and as a playwright, I want to retell her story with all of that terrible power I first encountered within it. I want to explore the elemental, the sexual, the mythic; attempt to free the characters from the straitjackets of being what Synge called 'saga people', to let them live and be as humans with all their terror and beauty; to make a version of this story which will resonate for audiences now, for people who may have no knowledge of the broader mythology or the literary tradition this new play would draw upon.

There's a universal and timeless power in the story of Deirdre and the Sons of Usna, and like all the great tales of love and betrayal there's an innate humanity and theatricality. Great stories deserve to be retold and reinterpreted; and perhaps Deirdre has not yet been seen in anything like her naked human potential – sexual, devious, innocent, passionate, complex – not just fated, beautiful, tragic.

A new Deirdre could be timely (the end of Tara for one thing), a modern telling of an old story to make young people sit up and take notice of the past.

One thing I know I don't want to do: 'create something quiet and stately and restrained'!

March 10:

Re-reading Synge's plays I'm amazed that no one was killed over the head of them. Mere audience riots seem mild when you consider how daring, how brave, how *true* they are. They might have killed someone if *The Tinker's Wedding* had been produced in Dublin when it was first written: mind you, that someone would probably have been Augusta Gregory - or some poor tinker reeling in the street.

For some reason I'm thinking about my first encounter with the 'Rejoyce and Synge Society' in Sydney abut fifteen years ago. I turned up a bit raw and idealistic, thinking they'd be interested in a young, living, aspiring writer. I had a bunch of small booklets of my own poems to sell and I noticed one young woman looking at them like they were compulsory smallpox samples. I don't think anyone actually bought one, though a few of the people there later became friends of mine. It was my first lesson in how Irish people abroad often don't want their literary or political certainties disturbed: dead poets can't talk back, living ones might say something unpleasant.

March 13:

Our neighbour, Mrs Lee, a widow and great friend to me in my youth, hated Synge. Whenever *Playboy* was broadcast on Radio Eireann she'd have a small paroxysm of indignation and anger. 'I can't stand listening to it,' – she'd mimic some mouthful of the language and shake her head. 'Is it any wonder the people went to America to get away from the likes of that?'

March 15:

Exactly two years since I saw Olivier Py's production of *Le Soulier de satin*, (*The Satin Slipper*) by Paul Claudel in Orléans. It was one of those profound experiences, almost religious, which occur now and again in a lifetime of theatre going (Tom Murphy's *Bailegangaire* was the first for me). *Soulier* was extraordinarily beautiful, funny, transcendent, dazzling the eye and the mind.

Something from that afternoon, from the play, from the music of it, seeped into the *Deirdre* I was writing. When I'd written a full draft we sent it to Py and word came back that he'd love to direct it. I went to see *Soulier* again in Paris that September and went back to Orléans the following April for Olivier's own play *Les Vainquers*. We hit it off right away; he'd gone to the Aran Islands when he was about twenty and went back to France to find somewhere similar to live, settling on Oeussant, an island off Brittany. Olivier said he was glad my *Deirdre* wasn't in the style of Synge. I said it couldn't be; I hope it's my style, me.

March 17:

I deliberately chose not to call my new play *Deirdre* as it was in early drafts, mainly to avoid confusion with the plays by Yeats and Synge. Despite this, confusion is created: I read that *A Cry From Heaven* is (quote) 'a version of *Deirdre of the Sorrows* by J.M. Synge', and am livid. The story is older than all of us – as Synge knew so well – and how could anyone have the temerity (or be stupid enough) to write *a version* of *his* play. The truth is that I feel Synge's *Deirdre* is the weakest of his plays, even allowing for the fact that it wasn't finished; and I'm not convinced by Yeats's contention that it would have been the playwright's 'masterwork' if he'd lived to complete it.

The language that soars and makes a new music in the other plays seems wrong here and contrived. Declan Kiberd argues that the writing is strongly influenced by Gaelic sources: written (*Oidhe Chloinne Uisnigh*) and oral (versions Synge *may* have heard on the Aran Islands); and says that this directness of approach is one reason why his play is more faithful to the legend and more exciting than the Yeats or Russell versions as drama. That's as may be but I can't believe in the spoken language of the play: this is the hard brutal world of Ulster, a different hardness to Galway or Kerry, a different way of saying and of being.

Every play must make its own language: we can't know how Deirdre, Naoise and Conor spoke (if their like ever existed, if they ever spoke at all). A play isn't a documentary and if it isn't free to re-imagine (that key word: *imagination*), to re-tell, to re-invent then one might as well not bother writing at all. As Synge said: 'People are entitled to use those old stories in any way they wish.'

I've read all the versions of the Deirdre story I know of: from *The Book of Leinster* and Geoffrey Keating's *Foras Feasa ar Éirinn* to oral versions in manuscript. I've assimilated them, forgotten them and made up my own. The ending of the play is mine – it won't be found in any source other than my brain and I make no apology for this. The language is mine – with all the risk (and I hope beauty) of poetic theatre – not Synge's 'peasant theatre' and not afraid of swords or ritual.

It's a bit like *At The Black Pig's Dyke*: I remember a few academics asking me what were the written sources for some of the images and myths in the play – and they were flummoxed when I said, in complete truth, that there weren't any. Henry Glassie's great book *All Silver and No Brass* and Alan Gailey's *Irish Folk Drama* were invaluable as regards mumming. But the rest came from oral tradition – from my parents and grandparents and god-knows who before them. And from me: my imagination, whatever you want to call the creative impulse.

March 18:

I notice that the original name for Rue des Irlandais is Rue du Cheval Vert, the Street of the Green Horse. The carved date has vanished after the century: 17... or maybe the number signifies an old quartier or district. There's an image of a white horse on the pavement just outside the Centre Culturel Irlandais, slightly faded, almost like a stencil or tattoo on the ground. But it's beautiful and gives me pleasure, this small white horse on Green Horse Street.

March 19:

Summer again. It's as if we've skipped spring and moved suddenly from winter snow to these days of heat and hurtful sunshine. In the cool of evening I take a wander and find the Panthéon transformed: a temporary garden of forty thousand jonquils, daffodils, created around the entrance and up the steps, being sold this weekend to raise funds for the Institut Curie and cancer research. Standing there I'm suddenly overwhelmed by a sense of grief at Synge's early death. I meander in tears remembering the story of the large wreath of daffodils sent by Annie Horniman for the funeral at Mount Jerome; and Yeats noting these and remembering that Synge had said he couldn't bear to look at a daffodil after enduring Miss Horniman's hectoring letters on yellow notepaper. Maybe it's because I've spent the day reading about him, but this moment seems like a kind of prayer: to stand and remember Synge here in the yellow light of flower and sun and to feel tears turn into a kind of ironic laughter; to walk slowly on the strip of artificial grass all the way down the pavement of the Rue Soufflot to the Luxembourg Gardens.

March 24:

Too wet to walk to Montparnasse cemetery to visit Beckett's grave. It had somehow seemed like the best way to mark the anniversary of Synge's death. Instead I stay in and browse again in the plays. It still pleases me to think *The Well of the Saints* was one of Beckett's favourite plays, that he may have been reading it in his last days. A few weeks ago José Férez K., who spent an afternoon in Paris smoking and drinking coffee with Beckett in the sixties after he'd directed *End Game* in England, told me that he sometimes goes and puts a cigarette on the grave. I like this simple act of remembrance. He also told me about his friend William Burroughs fronting up in Paris a bit the worse for wear, having written to Beckett to say he'd like to see him. Burroughs and a companion were ushered into the apartment, where Beckett was standing in profile in a twilight window. He never spoke to them, never said a word. But Burroughs' request had been granted - he did get to *see* Beckett. When the rain stops I get to see the grave: no cigarettes - a single red rose and three guitar plectrums. Maybe someone is confusing him with Jim Morrison … Even sodden tobacco seems more appealing.

March 30:

Most of the French people who know of Synge pronounce his name 'Singe'. I've come to like it: his work does still burn and always will. The more I think about it the more strongly I feel there should be some memorial to him here, and I go looking for one of the houses he gave as an address in between 1898 and 1902. The original building is gone and No 90 Rue d'Assas is now part of a big apartment block, functional and ugly, in what must have been a beautiful street a century ago. The building is diagonally opposite the Porte Assas entrance to the Luxembourg Gardens and up the street is the extraordinary red-brick building that houses the Institute of Arts and Architecture of the University of Paris. I stand looking at the eight storeys of apartments: smoked glass balconies, big windows, a few plants and bits of trees, occasional metal shutters and striped awnings. There's a basement car park with an apartment for rent just over the entrance. It could be anywhere, any city. The apartment block adjoins the equally drab Law and Economics Faculty of the University Pantheon-Assas. There's a squat glass and concrete affair selling drab books for these students – hard to make a bookshop ugly but this one succeeds.

So much of Paris intact and the one building you look for gone.

I reckon seven of the original buildings must have been knocked to make way for this progress. The first intact exterior is number 100, the Musée Zadkine, named for a Russian sculptor, Ossip Zadkine, who moved to Montparnasse in 1909. ('Come to see my crazy pad on Rue d'Assas and you'll see how a man's life can be changed by a pigeon loft, by a tree.') There's a plaque remembering him and his lover, Valentine Prax, a painter. I long for a plaque, a few words to acknowledge Synge's time in Paris. But not on this building. He deserves a better place to be remembered in a city he loved.

April 15

Rain again, then a clearance into sunlight and warmth. In the evening I finally locate 5 Rue Corneille, the address of the Hotel Corneille where Yeats and Synge met in 1896. I expect to find another modern block or something worse. Instead I find the building intact: no longer a hotel but intact. You'd walk by without another glance, another old Paris facade with its lives going on behind. Old rooms converted to apartments, maybe not so changed from the old hotel days. It's directly across the street from the side of the Odéon, almost certainly the street where the homeless couple were sleeping ten years ago. In 1896 Hotel Corneille must have been a simple boarding house: it was known as a place for the relatively less well-off traveller, a long way from Arthur Griffith's image of 'the decadent cynicism that passes current in the Latin Quartier.' Joyce stayed here when he first came to Paris in late 1902.

Number 3 Rue Corneillle next door is a bookshop – an elegant *literary* bookshop, Éditions Honoré Champion with its own imprint. In the window a lovely edition of Villon's *Lais, Testament, Poésies Diverses* with *Ballades en jargon*. The building that housed the famous Café Voltaire is just around the corner, across Rue Racine on the Place de l'Odéon. It was a haunt of Verlaine, Gide, Anatole France, and later the symbolist poets. They're here, all of them. And on this street between the Place Paul Claudel and the Place de l'Odéon two of our greatest writers met.

Here, in part, the genesis of our national theatre. This is the place for naming, for remembering, for a plaque. Some day their names must be written here, on the front of this modest building, here where all the streets are named for French dramatists.

I remember Yeats's funeral wreath for Synge: 'In memory of his gentleness and courage.' And Synge's translation of Villon's *Prayer of the old woman*:

> It's yourself that bore Jesus, that has no end of death, and he the Lord Almighty, that took our weakness and gave himself to sorrows, a young and gentle man. It's himself is our Lord surely, and it's in that faith I'll live always.

Illustration 6: A Wicklow Tramp. Synge Photo 6 TCD

6 | Driving Mrs Synge
By Sebastian Barry

One of the first place names to crop up in Synge's *In Wicklow*, Aughavanna, is just above me here in Moyne, a bit of a drive up a mountainy road; so when he names it, I suppose I think I know where it is. I have driven through it anyhow.

In Synge's time, Moyne would have been a very remote parish, but Aughavanna unimaginably so, for it is near nothing except itself. The condition of being near nowhere but where you are may confer remoteness, but it also went to make everywhere the centre of the world; which might be said to be a strong principle in Synge's plays, where the affairs of Mayo, Wicklow or the Islands are the affairs of world centres without rival.

The car has triumphed in erasure. It has erased Aughavanna, or at least the lost sense of victory it must have been in Synge's heart to reach it, wandering as he liked to do over these terrains, with his duck-gun or his fishing-rod.

Of course, for Synge the people hereabouts were peasants, not, as we would say, the people of the district, the population; but in his case the peasantry was an item to be looked at and talked with under a secret dispensation of equality, for the sake of unexpected information, and for information that could not be gleaned from his own set of people.

There is a sense in Synge's writing about Wicklow that not only did he by his own account learn the language of his plays through a crack in the floor of a house in Wicklow, which allowed him to overhear the servants; but that his own eyes, as he describes and itemizes, are a sort of crack between the world of the gentry and the peasant world.

He describes in an essay 'The People of the Glens' meeting a man on the road. 'Begging your pardon, sir,' says the man, 'I think you aren't Irish.' Synge tells him he is mistaken. But the man's point is that 'you don't speak the same as we do'; so that obviously for that man how you speak is your nationality, a thing that has vexed me also betimes. An old man in County Monaghan, as I quizzed him about the use of crushed whin-roots for ploughing horses (as you may do in Monaghan), said, 'I can talk to you because you are not Irish.' Well, that maybe is the opposite thing; or maybe not. In fact Synge's seeming otherness allows his vagrants and his old women to speak to him in a candid way – perhaps also with the freedom of invention not always given them in other exchanges with their own kin and kind. Or the freedom of elaborate linguistic expression itself – but always as a sort of courtly exchange, though which court would be hard to say. But definitely a high court. Because even if it is the 'poorest, lonesomest, wildest, dreariest bit of a hill', of course it is better to be there than anywhere else – unless it is New York. Kilpeddar for instance would be a dear place for scythes, so no good at all for habitation.

But I was thinking of my recent car journey with Mrs Margaret Synge to some of the places in Synge's plays and essays when I started this – this ramble. Though I carry no goosegun or fly rod. It was probably Synge that Yeats was thinking of when he was imagining a man, maybe twelve months since, going up a hillside for the fly-fishing. But I was thinking of Mrs Synge.

Margaret Synge came to Ireland first in the forties. She married a John Synge, who was not a playwright but played rugby for Ireland instead. John Synge sounds like he was a marvellous man. When he was at school in Bray, he was not good at the spelling; because he carried his famous uncle's name, he was mocked and beaten. Why could he not spell when his uncle was a great writer? Of course they didn't know Yeats himself was a terrible speller. So John Synge vowed he would call none of his sons John, to protect them, though John is a note sounding again and again along the long line, the long sentence of the Synges.

But anyway, his health was badly altered by malaria during his time in Nigeria – another version of Ireland and just as full of national briars. At the time of the Second World War he lay in a hospital in London and Margaret Synge was his nurse and against the rules – she tells me fearlessly – they fell in love. They used to sneak out of the hospital by separate doors in the wartime evenings. They might go into Piccadilly on the bus, John Synge's malaria still raging in him.

One night he spotted The Ritz open against the odds and they went in and had a drink. Margaret Synge still remembers sitting up at the bar in her fashionable coat – something like the inner tube of a tyre she says – and watching the crowd. It was her own crowd, but was it John Synge's own crowd? Maybe, maybe not. Fly-fishing at the Ritz possibly, engaging the natives – literally, in Margaret's case.

So then they came back to Ireland and settled in an old farmhouse in Ballinglen, in 1955 (the year of my birth, so I remember the detail). They had no money, and farmed strenuously, and raised three excellent sons. John Synge was the son of John Millington Synge's adored elder brother, Sam.

What I mean is, driving with Mrs Synge means of course that the Synges are still in Wicklow. She knows Wicklow better than many a Wicklow person (she is a Wicklow person of course). She will be showing me Lough Nahanagan for instance, which I had thought I didn't know, but will find I do after all; I just didn't know its *name* (a different matter). And Glanmore Castle above the Devil's Glen, the last great house the Synges inhabited, which was gutted and later rebuilt by an American. Or a German, I forget (this was only last week). She tells me that years after the place was sold, John learned that the penultimate owner, his uncle I think, asked John's father if he might like to take over Glanmore. His father, never mentioning it to John, thought not. And though John loved Glanmore, Margaret says she thinks his father was right, he would have worried himself to death over the place. Worry is a great destroyer of people and houses certainly, and artists for that matter. Synge had a lot of worry conferred on him by the pundits of Dublin, respectable and not respectable.

The fortunes of Glanmore in the matter of Synges were already in trouble during the time of Pestalozzi John (this may be the wrong spelling, but we are in an aural world in my ancient Saab), who died in 1846 (so says his stone in the Synge church). When the pride of the Synges, a young captain, was killed in the First World War, something went out of the song of the Synges, and Glanmore fell away eventually. The last owner, the daughter of John's uncle, had a fear that one of the towers of the house was going to fall into the Devil's Glen; the fear grew like an illness and she sold the house to rid herself of the fear.

We drive to the gates of Castle Kevin, another old Synge-associated property, because Synge's mother used to rent it in the summer, bringing all her goods and chattels in a cart along the road from Greystones or Glenageary. Synge himself as a young man would have knocked about its avenues. It is owned now by Daniel Day-Lewis and his wife Rebecca Miller, daughter of Arthur.

It seemed a strange place, deep in drips of rain, in drapes of nameless weeds. We didn't dare go up the inner avenue, but turned back down to the gates when we saw a fierce man staring at us. He didn't seem to know a Synge when he saw one. He probably knew the Barrys were low types from the hills, Kelshabeg, or even Aughavanna. But there was a wintry sadness hanging in that avenue, very netherworldly and stark. It was the next day I read in the newspaper that Arthur Miller, the last great playwright of that other western world, had died that very day in Connecticut, with his family around him.

I used to worry that Synge may have died without ever kissing his girl, but I was relieved to have that quietly contradicted by Mrs Synge. Of course it was a foolish thought. I asked her how his mother felt about her son going out with an actress, and an Irish Catholic actress to boot. I can't remember what she said.

When Synge is mentioned, I always hear Tom Murphy, one of the greatest living Irish playwrights, saying that Synge was the master, Synge 'the finest of us all'. And yet it is easy to forget how long long ago Synge flourished, how long long ago he died. Margaret talks about Pestalozzi John as if he had died maybe in the forties, the nineteen forties; so maybe it is a Synge characteristic that they, each of them, seem present and correct in all ages.

Well, they all live there in the heaven of Margaret Synge's memory. I have to confess here I think Margaret Synge a heavenly person. Her decorum is musical. Her composure is inspiring. Her friendship is to be hoarded. Maybe old/young/eternal John Millington Synge was like that. I suspect so. His brother Sam loved him, always a good sign. Although he preferred to ignore the fact that his brother had connections with the dubious world of the theatre.

It may be strange now to think Synge was fallen upon by the commentators of his day for the use of the word 'shift' in a play. What he actually wrote was (Christy speaking):

> It's Pegeen I'm seeking only, and what'd I care if you brought me a drift of chosen females, standing in their shifts itself, maybe, from this place to the eastern world.

The 'maybe' is good.

Of course, the whole play is perfect and brilliant. It is language (the language he didn't speak, the language he heard with his eyes) gone to heaven, and emerged as the Elizabethan tongue of elaborate angels. There is no limit to the elaboration of the speeches, the nuts in them, or the joy, the thing he emphasized that plays must have (I feel bad about my own plays when I read that. I suppose he is right). The exuberance of Christy's words is of a brain that has ten thousand dancers in his head, and all of them in their shifts, and no 'maybe' about it.

Well, at last Margaret brings me – directs me – to Lough Nahanagan. (Before I forget, Rathvanna, mentioned in *The Tinker's Wedding* and elsewhere, is an invented name, she says, quite a rare thing, if not singular, for Synge). Lough Nahanagan is one of the places, Synge says (in his book), where a language is spoken 'more Elizabethan than the English of Connaught'. The other places he mentions in this respect are Aughavanna (just up the hill, as I said, I must go there some day and stop and see if they still do speak that English. I doubt it), Glenmalure, where my own people, Dunnes and Cullens, were peasants over seven generations at least, and whose language I certainly learned as a child, and sits deep in my tongue to this day (I hope and pray).

But Lough Nahanagan is not so far from The Seven Churches as it happens. It is a region of mortarless walls, deserted lead mines and the like, and a river, and a fine, well a wonderful, waterfall, down which Margaret Synge tells me a lady fell to her death. I ask her if she committed suicide, but Margaret says she didn't think so, though she might have pulled her chair too close to the falls with something vague in mind. Otherwise, apart from thoughts of that lady, there is no one about except a few very cold tourists, who might even be Irish, but everyone is a tourist up here, except Margaret. (Her old map across her lap has pencil markings on it that turn out to have been written there by her father years ago. It is a wonderful rare map, with all sorts of secret information on it that the world will never know. Such maps are extinct.) Even Lough Nahanagan is not quite 'at home', at least it is invisible from the road. It is said there are good trout up there, if crazy in the head, and I can believe it. But they must be lonely. It is fearsomely lonely. There are no people going about speaking a language 'more Elizabethan than the English of Connaught'. There is no one at all to call Synge, or Mrs Synge, or even myself, a foreigner.

Synges themselves are few on the ground, although we do stand later on sacred ground, 'the Synge paddock' as Margaret calls it, a little Victorian enclosure where Synges lie in the Synge churchyard, including her marvellous John. 'I'll be lying in there,' she says, pointing to some unpromising dockleaves, and I ask her of her kindness to stay alive at least another twenty years, if only for my sake (I am selfish in my friendships and care nothing for anyone else). She says she will, and she will likely keep her word.

It is the word of a Synge. Fifteen thousand words of a Synge made the greatest play in the Irish canon, *The Playboy of the Western World*. It is a very nice thing that the Western world he refers to is actually Mayo, where once I lived myself. I always think of Mayo as a little Northern (not Connemara, not Galway, the traditional West). It could have been *The Playboy of the North Western World*. His other plays, apart from *Riders to the Sea*, are set in Wicklow, in the 'eastern world' of Christy's speech. And I think it is true that they all speak the same, the characters, so it is a very democratic language, and he has bestowed his discoveries in language on the entire nation, as if that English he heard through the floor in Wicklow were really an Irish – a National tongue. Even the ancient grandees in *Deirdre of the Sorrows* speak the same language. It is a measure of Synge's elegant love, that he could fish such a language up from a Wicklow kitchen and spread it all over the country.

We go into the church and Mrs Synge shows me the stone that remembers the death of young Captain Synge. The Fall of the House of Synge, she calls it, but it is one of her singing pleasantries. The house of Synge is quite eternally alive. The people are gone from Lough Nahanagan, and the tinkers from Ballinaclash, and even Rathvanna, that never existed; The Beauty of Ballinacree is gone, Sarah Casey herself, they are gone from the lonely glens and the back roads of Rathdangan, where Synge saw the Tinkers gathered every year to choose a yearly wife. The descendants of those Travellers used to come up our own farmyard and rattle the latch on Sarah Cullen and Annie Dunne, and frighten the life out of us children. That's how it was in those times, and I have written about it without ever thinking till this moment that I lived as a little boy of four in the land and the language of Synge. I write this little rambling essay here under those very mountains, of Kiltegan, Ninevah and Kelsha. All those people are gone, my own included, but the house of Synge will never be gone. For it is a house made of such words that no wind can touch it, government disdain it, or mortal life leave it empty.

Illustration 7: Riders to the Sea, 1906, with Maire O'Neill, Sara Allgood and Brigit O'Dempsey. TCD MS 6198/15

7 |. Locus Pocus: Synge's Peasants

Mary O'Malley

Synge's Aran, I read. Synge's peasants. Picasso's women. Lorca's Andalucia.

This is a reader's response to one playwright and two plays, without a reader's distance. If I am a writer whose imagination is now weaned, as Seamus Heaney so aptly puts it, from my origins, those origins are important to me not alone as the locus of so much of my work and my self, but because they are the site of the peasant idiom so famously employed by John Millington Synge, whose ear was very finely tuned and who often got it technically as well as dramatically right. And while the writer's imagination is weaned from her origins, the writer never is.

I grew up in a welter of lobster pots and nets and currachs being tarred. I played in the upside down cathedral of one half – the stem – of a cut-in-two pucan. This had been put in a field out of sight of the sea. The other half was for the hens, and covered in bird droppings as thickly as Alcatraz, though no magenta flowers grew on our unyielding climate. I was taken out in a currach very young and I loved the green swell of it, the massive oxen of a deep current, Lorca's 'buey de agua' sensed beneath the surface. I learned how to sit still and not ask questions while the men talked. I felt safe. I knew the sea could turn.

As a young child I picked carrageen and picked spuds and salted fish. All these activities were carried out in the cold lash of April, or the bitter wind of November, so the body's memory insists. I know the salting was actually done in summer, the minute the fish were gutted and washed. This task I also carried out, when I was old enough to be trusted with a knife. My fingers were thin and they reddened and froze more quickly than anybody else's, I was nervous and lacked dexterity so I did all of these things badly, but as the eldest I had to show some sort of example.

While we were not as dependent on the sea as an island would be, we depended on it for sustenance, for beauty and for escape to America. The sea was capricious. The ability to predict weather had to be matched by the ability to know where and when the fish were to be found, as well as how to catch them. The sea could be miserly, ensuring a winter of want and poverty, or it could, without warning, be lavish.

As in fishing villages the world over, the men were either 'out on sea' or the currachs were in. When I was nine or ten the family moved to a house with a view of the quay and my father got a bigger boat, a twenty eight footer, the 'Grainne Mhaol'. The dominance of the sea was then complete; I depended on it for dreams.

The season was short, the winters long and life often brutal. In summer, the boats went out and money came in. If weather threatened or the boat was late, one of us children would be sent down to the pier head to look over the stormwall and scan the grey for a sight of the boat. If there was further cause for concern, a fast child was sent to see if anything could be spotted from further along the shore and finally – and I only remember this happening half a dozen times – someone was dispatched to see if the men had landed in the next village, and if not, whether anyone else was in. The fears were never voiced, but even the youngest child felt the tension – we learned it with our prayers.

Aillbebrack in the nineteen-fifties and early sixties was far closer to the world of Synge's *Aran Islands* than it was to Dublin or to the Galway of today. This small village at the edge of the Atlantic in the area was known to outsiders as Connemara, but to people from other parts of the region, and to us, it was known as Errismor.

Such knowledge, or lack of it, was one of the many small signifiers that told us whether someone was a stranger or not. Another was how they spoke. Not alone the accent, but more importantly the use of the telltale phrase. Even the children in every locality in Ireland could, before television, tell who came from within its borders and who from without after a few minutes of conversation.

The history of a people works on their language; the language limits what they can express of their world. When a language is lost in the place to which it is native, the effects are by definition more extreme than when this happens because of migration or immigration. This part of Connemara spoke an English not alone wedded to its deeper Irish grammatical structure, but moulded into a shape that could to some extent express the place and history of those who lived, and lost, in it. 'The limits of our language are the limits of our world', Wittgenstein says. For ourselves, or for others? This is, in some ways central to how I read Synge, and to the critical essays and commentaries that I have read about him.

My grandmother and parents, my uncles and the neighbours spoke an English that was far from standard. 'We're going out after the pots' or 'He's over after the cattle' or 'Think will herself be looking for more flour?' 'I hear there was great gaisce altogether at Taimin over in Keogh's.' 'By the cross of Christ, I'll lay that fella out with a kick' would not be out of the question. Such language is easy to exaggerate and it is no surprise that Synge lost the run of himself in *The Playboy*.

There is a very clear line between parody and poetry, but the ear has to be finely tuned to the idiom and every nuance to achieve one and avoid the other. Daniel Corkery has described this linguistic minefield more than adequately in his *Synge and Anglo Irish Literature*, and I think that in essence he is right. He also says, to paraphrase wildly, that as a Protestant in love with the notion of the wild natural man, Synge didn't understand the nature and place of Catholicism, and this lack of understanding led him astray in *The Playboy*. Corkery is referring to the use of profanity, certain aspects of the overtly sexual talk and behaviour in the play that cause it to be read as parody, if not insult.

In other words, when Synge wanted pagan, he saw only pagan. He intended not to insult but to express what he saw as the great sport and heroics of the unfettered peasant. But the peasant world was guided by one god with two sets of saints and two kinds of knowledge, the old and the Roman. There was little direct conflict between the two.

As a child, I never gave any thought to the fact that our three main saints, Brigid, Cailin and Mac Dara were never on the calendar. I knew St Patrick wasn't either and if I thought about it at all, I put it down to them being somehow native because St Patrick, wherever he was from, is legitimized by the same type of half heroic story as the other three, and all gave their names to known places.

Synge wrote *The Playboy* in a ferment of sexual frustration, and it shows. When he arrived in Inis Meain at the age of twenty-seven with a sack of books and a broken heart, he had an eye for the beauty of the girls, and they must have had great sport with him on an island well out in the Atlantic at the end of the nineteenth century.

When I first read *The Playboy* sometime in my teens I thought it was ridiculous. I was mildly offended, not at anything in the play, but that educated people thought it had something to say about the kind of life lived by my ancestors and their like. A few girls in my class immediately adopted several phrases from the play's rich store and used them at every opportunity, as young girls will. Everything that girls could be doing in the long evenings after Samhain they would be accusing one another of doing, from 'eating a bit in one house and drinking a sup in another, like an old braying jackass' to 'squeezing kisses on the puckered lips' of whoever was that week's object of desire.

We loved Shaneen Keogh, he was such a slieveen, and a boy was instantly, and unanimously, nicknamed in his honour. We thought Pegeen Mike was alright, if a bit rough. We didn't know what to make of the Widow Quin, but none of that mattered, because no woman in her right mind would be so desperate for a man that she would have the Playboy, 'even if he was served up on a plate with sauce', much less take him seriously. Then it got more ridiculous – the great deed that made a hero out of him was killing his father? And as for two women fighting over him ... *seafóid*. We couldn't see why grown women and a number of men had to take Christy Mahon making an eejit out of himself seriously, or why we had to do it over three acts.

We had learned about the willing suspension of disbelief, but this was a step too far. We knew, though there would have been no need to articulate it, that killing a father could be a sin and a tragedy, but it could never be taken as the basis for comedy. It seemed insulting, that such a man could be presented as serious, what kind of fools did people take us for? Noble fools, in Synge's case.

We couldn't see what the rioting was about, though we supposed that Dublin people must be easily shocked. Maybe they were Protestants and of a higher sensibility? Not even the nuns were shocked by the drift of chosen females in their shifts. That image only struck us because it was versatile. Nuns still wore habits then and were just about to uncover their hair. Since rumour was rife about whether they had any at all, the picture of a drift of them in slips or nightdresses was too good to resist. As for the hero, even someone as desperate as we supposed young nuns to be wouldn't think much of the Playboy, and even nuns knew Shaneen Keogh was more of a failed priest than a man.

Young girls, as the agony aunt Angela McNamara remarked once in a radio interview, can be very bold. Synge was taken with such boldness, but I don't believe he understood that boldness was legislated for by a mixture of religious rules and marriage prospects that brooked no disobedience if a girl wanted to retain her good name. Good name, like virginity, could never be recovered and soiled goods were not wanted. The rules of behaviour might be different from those in his

Protestant Dublin world, but there were rules and they were clear to the locals if not to him.

There is no evidence in any of the plays that Synge knew or cared about the quick slip that could lead to disgrace, nor the consequences of it. But the girls knew, and this kind of gap can lead to mistakes in interpretation. No father hoping to marry a daughter to the likes of Shaneen Keogh would leave her in the presence of a strange man at night, much less one whose seed, breed and generation were unfamiliar. All this we girls took in at a glance during the late sixties, when our lives and our society were balanced on the cusp of change. Things of a sexual nature were never mentioned directly; it was all hint, allegation and giggling embarrassment. But girls are bold at that age.

The close connection between the black ram, the Widow Quin's breast and the bishop disgusted as much as it mystified. Not even the explicit passages where Diarmuid lay with Grainne in the Toraiocht, and there is no getting away from it in middle Irish, were passed over as swiftly by the nuns as some of the more outlandish speeches in *The Playboy*. Anything in literature that causes a nun major embarrassment sticks in the mind forever, but I have no memory of this passage from my schoolgirl reading. It bothers me now, because there is an authentic spite in the accusation, as the exact register of Christy's 'God save you kindly' prevents me enjoying the play as a gaudy romp with purple interludes and awakens, in Corkery's words, ancestral disturbances. My disturbances are neither nationalistic nor religious. They have to do with language and cultural appropriation.

Certain places exercise such a powerful force on the creative imagination that they become territorially attractive to artists. I grew up in such a place. It became clear to me at a young age that the outside world had little interest in what locals thought, and that by and large the increasing numbers of visitors had no interest in us beyond the provision of local colour.

As I read more widely, and began to read literary criticism at University, I was disappointed to see that this lack of curiosity applied also to academics, though that was not really surprising.

After all, better to work out your theories on the blank canvas of a real landscape inhabited, if at all, by idealized stereotypes than to risk the awkward answer, the dissenting word of the actual people themselves.

The people themselves were not represented in English. I found wonder and joy in literature in English, but I only encountered my own world in the stories of Ó Flatharta and Ó Direáin, Ó Cadhain. The poetry worked on another level, and it gave me some small permission, but the prose legitimized the world I came from, though all I knew then, or needed to know, was the right sort of ease and unease. 'They gave me permission', as Seamus Heaney so accurately put it, referring to his early reading of Kavanagh, 'to dwell without anxiety among the cultural landmarks of my life'. In literature, I only glimpsed the world I knew second-hand in the English in which I was raised.

Some years ago, when I read Tim Robinson's brilliant and cogent introduction to *The Aran Islands* (and why – since he himself so clearly states the obvious: that all introductions reduce 'the dimensionality' of what they introduce – was this not published as an afterword?) I gleaned a great deal about the intellectual concerns of the author and several sharp insights into Synge's overheated passion for the actress Molly Allgood. My schoolgirl reading would have been well served by the clear chronological detail, and the geographical information, but the cultural contextualization in this or any other critical work would have done me no good at all.

The questions we pose about a society we are outside of can be useful or they can be irrelevant. The answers, should we be so brave as to offer them, will always tell more about their author than about that society. The world Synge wrote about in both *The Playboy* and *Riders to the Sea* is essentially the world I grew up in, defined by the two great signifiers of that world: speech and the sea. This was the peasant idiom that Synge, perhaps uniquely, has mastered and it is therefore impossible for me to read him with the disinterested attention of the critic or academic. I will always see or read Synge's plays and, by

definition, critical commentary on them, through the particular
lens of my place and background.

Riders to the Sea plays equally well in English and in Irish. It
would, I have little doubt, play as well in a good translation of
Greek, Italian or Spanish and it would certainly play well in
Portuguese. This is a near perfect play, 'a tiny epiphany' as an
Aran man told me. It is Synge the poet at his magnificent best.
The play is short. Its theatrical brilliance lies in making the
realism of the set serve as an altar for the ritual objects and
actions surrounding death by sea, the purgatorial vigil while the
mother waits for her son's body to be found, then the relief of
a funeral, a grave to go to. Maurya is Everymother. This is real
life pared down, simple objects invested with their full
symbolic power. It has the measure and comfort of a Latin rite,
a rare event when poetry and drama are one, the rhythm of the
speech underpinning the action and driving the momentum
towards its perfect – and inevitable – conclusion.

When Maurya says of the young priest : 'Tis little the like of
him knows of the sea ... Bartley will be lost now ... ', she
speaks with the perfectly pitched authority of dream. The
priest, saying God would not leave her ' destitute, with no son
living', speaks with the distant authority of Rome and she pays
him no heed. Here is a perfect rendering of the balance struck
between faith and fatalism, a balance absent from most of the
other plays. 'If it's meant for you, it'll follow you.' This is still
said of death by drowning.

A musician I know says every human being can survive a
specific number of renditions of the song 'The Fields of
Athenry'. It is important to know your decreed number,
because one too many will kill you. He has forty, so he takes
great care to limit his exposure. I feel like that about *The
Playboy*.

Garry Hynes's famous first production of it and the gleeful
savagery of Maeliosa Stafford's Christy and Marie Mullen's
Widow Quin did something to convert me. The relish with
which the words were spoken, down to even the most
cringingly embarrassing of the love talk, drew me in. The best
conversations I have had about the play are with actors. In

their world, the language has become the main character and while I have come to enjoy its extravagance it will forever be a language adrift from its moorings. *Riders to the Sea* is language raised to a higher power. In *The Playboy*, 'they' are using 'our' language. *Riders to the Sea* is written in everyone's language, and wherever it places itself, its poetry cannot be divorced from its origins.

Illustration 8: Synge with his mother, Rosie Calthrop (centre), and Annie Harmar, in the summer of 1900. TCD MS 6198/6

8 | Apart from Anthropology
Anthony Cronin

The creative process thrives on ambiguities and indeed apparent contradictions. Criticism is often surprisingly less happy with them afterwards. In the case of John Millington Synge certain ambiguities which were at the mainspring of his creative urge have had an unsettling effect on criticism; and made him the victim of confusions about the relationship of his life to his art – and of Irish life to his art – which still prevent us from assessing his achievement dispassionately and perhaps celebrating it as we should.

He has not on the whole been well served by his critics, and perhaps even less so by his partisans. He had the misfortune first of all to have a man of supreme genius as an ally and indeed as an impresario, making as is usual an impresario's inaccurate claims. Yeats was a great theorist of art and artistry but he wrote criticism only in snatches and as an addendum to theory. Of the three essays included in *The Cutting of an Agate*, the first, the preface to *The Well of the Saints*, reminds us of the famous exhortation to 'Go to the Aran Islands. Live there as if you were one of the people themselves; express a life that has never found expression' – and we are back with Synge as the anthropologist-naturalist and all the dreary quarrels, from the *Playboy* row down to the present day, about his accuracy in the plays as a describer of folk-life and Irish peasant character, the endless arguments about whether he was, on the one hand,

traducer, or, on the other, idealizer. In the same essay Yeats
goes on to say:

> He went to Aran and became a part of its life, living upon salt
> fish and eggs, talking Irish for the most part, but listening also
> to the beautiful English which has grown up in the Irish
> speaking districts, and takes its vocabulary from the time of
> Malory and of the translators of the bible, but its idiom and its
> vivid metaphor from Irish. When Mr. Synge began to write in
> this language, Lady Gregory had already used it finely in her
> translations of Dr. Hyde's lyrics and plays, or of old Irish
> literature, but she had listened with different ears.

This too perpetuates argument and, worse, confusion.
'Kiltartan' is still, quite properly, a dirty word in certain circles;
and although Yeats, with his usual percipience, almost cuts out
the confusions he has already raised when he adds, 'He made
his own selection of word and phrase, choosing what would
express his own personality', he has still said enough to invite,
in the course of time, retorts such as that of the strictly urban-
minded Myles na Gopaleen who declared:

> A lifetime of cogitation has convinced me that in this Anglo-
> Irish literature of ours (which for the most part is neither
> Anglo, Irish, nor literature) nothing in the whole galaxy of fake
> is comparable with Synge ... The trouble probably began with
> Lever and Lover. But I always think that in Synge we have the
> virus isolated and recognizable ... It is not that Synge made
> people less worthy or nastier, or even better than they are, but
> he brought forward amusing clowns talking a sub-language of
> their own and bade us take them very seriously. There was no
> harm done there, because we have long had the name of having
> heads on us. But when the counterfeit bauble began to be
> admired outside of Ireland by reason of its oddity and 'charm',
> it soon became part of the literary credo here that Synge was a
> poet ... a bit of a genius indeed ... And now the curse has
> come upon us, because I personally have met in the streets of
> Ireland persons who are clearly out of Synge's plays. They talk
> and dress like that and damn the drink they'll swally but the
> mug of porter in the long nights after Samhain.

What Myles is saying is slightly different from what Oscar
Wilde said: according to Myles, life imitates bad art; but it is

noteworthy that Synge is also getting the blame for the sort of intellectual stage Irishness which undoubtedly has been the bane of much of our literature since independence. In effect, Myles says, Synge raised the tone of stage-Irishism, and made it acceptable in more or less nationalist literary circles. Nationalism, or at least the more nationalistic kind of writer, having attacked the Synge-song to begin with, ended by apparently adopting it. The appeal of the picturesque triumphed over the ideal of purity; an ideal strangeness was more important than an ideal sexlessness.

This is perhaps why the *Playboy* riots now seem so far away. Synge's brief moment (1902 to 1909) coincided with the rebirth of a kind of nationalism which was guilty of distortions in the interests of the ideal; but, if it is now a long time in fact, it is an even longer stretch in terms of fashion since Arthur Griffith attacked the *Playboy* as a libel on Irish womanhood and five hundred policemen were needed to keep order within and without the theatre.

But the row was one after Yeats's own heart; and he continued to rub it in. In the third essay in *The Cutting of an Agate*, 'J.M. Synge and the Ireland of his Time', the poet who was to found a whole aesthetic on the idea of art as the creation of exalted, noble images for contemplation, claimed that the 'lyric beauty', the 'violent laughter' etc. of the *Playboy* were all taken straight out of peasant Ireland. At the time this was written he was annoying the peasants and their literary embodiers and spokesmen further, but of course, given that they were to pin their faith also to the idea of exalted, noble images, even if mostly in the somewhat degraded form of the picturesque, it would not be long until they came his way. Twenty years after that essay, Daniel Corkery, in what was long a seminal book, *Synge and Anglo-Irish Literature*, was to argue also that Synge's importance was the depth of his knowledge of the people and to declare flatly:

> Here, by one stroke, to show how he stands apart from all his fellow writers, it is but necessary to state that he, an ascendancy man, went into the huts of the people and lived with them.

'An ascendancy man.' He takes back what he gives; but what he gives has proved fatal enough also. Soon, by a supreme historical irony, Synge's defenders were among the lovers of the peasant-picturesque, the remnants of the old Abbey and Radio Eireann gang, the lineal descendants of the nationalists of 1907 (the only difference being that they substituted one kind of noble savage for another): his enemies among the cosmopolitans, the urbanites, the sophisticates like Myles. The charge of being an ascendancy man who distorted and condescended by reason of that fact was dropped by one side and revived by the other. It was a sentimental literary idealization which was now charged against him, not a libel or a travesty.

Yet that he was 'an ascendancy man' is undeniable: the point to be made, if any point must, being that this particular ambiguity or contradiction was more important to him as a man turning his life-experiences, contradictions and ambiguities into art, than it is to us. Synge was in fact sprung from the narrowest, most bigoted, bible-thumping, proselytizing, peasant-despising while yet peasant-exploiting kind of Protestant, ascendancy, landlord stock. Yet he fell in love with the Catholic 'natives'. He tramped the roads of Wicklow and West Kerry; he went to the Islands; he learnt the language; he listened at chinks in the floorboards. And he wrote *The Tinker's Wedding*, *The Well of the Saints* and *The Playboy of the Western World*, 'travesties' according to the most fervent and patriotic of the natives then. Marvellous illuminations of a life undreamed-of according to urban sophisticates. The irony being, of course, that it was the urban sophisticates who accused him of ridiculous distortions and indeed idealizations; while it was the most peasant-minded and patriotic (in the literary sense anyway) who stuck by him, believing (correctly as it happens) that their own importance depended entirely on whether the poetic peasant existed and whether the contemplation of his life had marvellous illuminations to offer the rest of us.

It is therefore Synge's misfortune that his secondary, or what might even be called his background, subject, the life of the Gaelic West, still obscures what is perhaps his real subject, his

real achievement and his claim to lasting fame. Of course there
is no doubt that it was his entrancement with the people of
Aran, of the Wicklow glens, and of West Kerry that set fire to
his imagination and released his real theme. True creation, art as
opposed to any other kind of statement, is a matter of
embodiment. And there can be no doubt in the mind of anyone
who reads those sad, yet celebratory and noble books, *The Aran
Islands* and *In Wicklow and West Kerry*, in which a dying man
contemplates with the brooding intensity of genius the
remnants of an immemorial but already dying culture, that
Synge found himself and found embodiments for his real theme
in the poor, barren and beautiful places of Ireland. In passage
after passage he reveals not only insight, but his love and his
personal emotion. Thus, on Inishmaan after a night of storm,
he writes:

> The continual passing in this island between the misery of last
> night and the splendour of today, seems to create an affinity
> between the moods of these people and the moods of varying
> rapture and dismay that are frequent in artists, and in certain
> forms of alienation. Yet it is in the intonation of a few
> sentences or some old fragment of melody that I catch the real
> spirit of the island.

In West Kerry, near Dunquin, he watches the people wending
their way to mass on a Sunday morning,

> the men in homespun and the women wearing blue cloaks, or,
> more often, black shawls twisted over their heads. This
> procession along the olive bogs, between the mountains and the
> sea, on this grey day of autumn, seemed to wring me with the
> pang of emotion one meets everywhere in Ireland – an emotion
> that is partly local and patriotic, and partly a share of the
> desolation that is mixed everywhere with the supreme beauty of
> the world.

And he had, whatever simple people may have said
afterwards under pressure from Dublin enemies retailing stories
of scandalous plays performed far away, the gift of friendship
and sympathy; with the young, with the very old, and – perhaps
this is the most significant thing of all – with the women. Over
and over again he speaks of the beauty of the Island women in

their red dresses against the bare rock, of their singularly beautiful faces, of their openness, frankness, and simplicity.

As an anthropologist-naturalist, then, or whatever it may be proper to call him, Synge was, in the prose books at least, not an inconsiderable observer, though naturally he saw all that he did through the light of his own predestined imagination. But critics who have concentrated, as for extraneous political and other reasons they have, on the contradictions inherent in the spectacle of this scion of the ascendancy as the writer of peasant plays are wasting everybody's time. Whatever Synge may have said during the stress of the *Playboy* riots, however sedulously critics, including Robin Skelton in *The Writings of J.M. Synge*, may search for the origins of his plots in his experiences in the West of Ireland and in Wicklow, these are not primarily naturalistic plays. The mob who gleefully hooted 'Lynchehaun' at the author in the Abbey were right. (Synge had tried to justify the probability of his play by reference to a dubiously existent murderer of that name who he said had been hidden by the people of Erris.) It illuminates matters here to remember that Synge lived in the era when the 'problem play' was dominant. Naturalistic drama with a social theme was the accepted mode. People expected it and they looked for it. It therefore also illuminates matters to remember the surprising fact that Synge and Chekhov were almost contemporaries. Chekhov was of course interested in what was happening to the Russian soul; he was interested in the Russian character; he was interested in social change. Synge had all these interests too, so far as the people of the West were concerned, but both were vastly more interested in primary themes of their own. Synge had really only one, and he was probably prepared to throw naturalism and social accuracy overboard to some extent at least to get it. What was it?

When we realize what it is, when we 'isolate' it from the other questions, we go far to restore Synge to his proper place among writers of any nationality; and that is a high one the present writer has no doubt.

Unfortunately, however, when we make the attempt we come up against further contradictions and ambiguities in the relationship of the man to his work which have been and are the source of critical confusions also, for critics have touched on these too, and again mostly as if they somehow invalidate the work, when in fact they may illuminate it. At least from 1897 on, Synge was a sick, indeed, to be brutal about it, a dying man. Yet the work glorifies health, vitality, licence, vigour. Further, he was reserved, introspective, almost silent in most sorts of company. Yeats described him as being one of those sorts of artists who have little personality, as far as the casual eye can see, little personal will, but a fiery and brooding imagination. I cannot imagine him anxious to impress or convince in any company, or saying more than was sufficient to keep the talk circling.

Yet the plays are full of talkers, spellbinders, liars, eloquent chancers of all descriptions. (Christy Mahon is by no means the only one.) Furthermore, as Skelton and before him Greene and Edward M. Stephens in the official biography made clear – Maurice Bourgeois was the first to hint at it – Synge was an unhappy lover who had had at least two serious rejections of affection before he began his final relationship with the Abbey actress Molly Allgood. The first and most serious of these, by Cherrie Matheson, was on religious grounds. Synge had declared himself an atheist, and she, the daughter of the leader of the Plymouth Brethren, regarded this, however she may have felt about him, as an insuperable obstacle. When finally, only four years before his death, he met the nineteen-year-old Molly, he had the good or ill fortune to find the sort of girl who kept a man in uncertainties of all descriptions. The portrait by John B. Yeats in the Dublin National Gallery which Skelton reproduces and the photograph which also appears in his book show her for what she was: a beautiful, high-spirited, intelligent girl, full of vitality, but wilful and stubborn to a degree. Pegeen Mike of *The Playboy* in fact.

In *J.M. Synge and his World* Skelton quotes a passage from a draft of Synge's first play, *When the Moon has Set*:

> My life has gone to ruin because I misunderstood love and because I was scrupulous when I should have been strong. I treated women as if they were gods and they treated me as if I

might be damned for their amusement. If you love a woman
subdue her.

And when one reads all the plays together, one is struck by a
strange fact. Synge has really only one primary theme: the
ironies, and in particular the verbal ironies, of the relationships
of men and women. To make this assertion is certainly not to
demean him, for the theme is, to say the least, an important
one. To add that, apart from Shakespeare in certain of the
comedies, he is the greatest dramatist to have handled it in the
English language is to do no more than give him his due.

His first play, *Riders to the Sea*, is something of an aberration
in the corpus of his work. Skelton praises it for its mythic
elements; and it has been held up to admiration as classical
tragedy in miniature. Criticism is generally pleased to have such
matters to discuss, but the truth is that *Riders to the Sea* is a
contrived solemnity by a writer who had not yet found himself.
Even so there are glimmerings of his themes, albeit 'tragic'
rather than comic ones, for the point is the relationship of
women who wait and mourn with the men whose devouring
mistress is the sea.

In *The Shadow of the Glen*, written more or less concurrently,
and *The Tinker's Wedding* his primary subject is clearer to his
audience, as it was perhaps to himself also, and from now until
the end, even in the tragic Deirdre, he will not relinquish it. In
The Shadow of the Glen Nora picks Michael to supplant her ageing
husband with a degree of clear-sightedness and a degree of
contempt, simply, she claims, because he is a man, passable and
available; and because, like her husband, he has money. At the
same time she pays the oblique compliment of a claim that her
standards in men are high:

> … if it's a power of men I'm after knowing they were fine men,
> for I was a hard child to please, and a hard girl to please, and it's
> a hard woman I am to please this day, Michael Dara, and it's no
> lie I'm telling you.

After all of which she goes off with the tramp, leaving both
and embittered husband and a bewildered Michael behind her,

and advancing as her reason one worthy of a later heroine in the statement that the tramp has, after all, 'a fine bit of talk'.

The long-debated question, also raised by the conduct of later heroines, as to whether women or men have more regard for convention, and respect for the bonds of marriage, is the central theme of *The Tinker's Wedding*. Of course Sarah wants marriage, even though, as her husband reminds her, she has been going beside him a long time and reared a lot of children. Of course Michael is, being a man, resistant to the idea. So far Synge does not differ from the consensus of male writers on the theme.

But Sarah also wants a continued freedom to assure herself that her powers of attraction are not lost, a need which the majority of male writers have, from the dawn of time, attributed unhesitatingly to the male. And in the end it is her primal realism, not Michael's, which prevails over the marriage idea and dismisses it and the respectability which goes with it as less important than the price to be paid.

But neither *The Shadow of the Glen* nor *The Tinker's Wedding* are truly more than curtain-raisers; and it is on the two great plays that followed that Synge's reputation must finally rest. *The Well of the Saints* mixes so many elements – the eternal conflict of illusion and reality, wish and fulfilment; the meaninglessness of human existence compared with the human being's capacity to feel and to suffer; the contrast between the riches of absolute poverty and the deprivations of partial possession – that it is easy to miss its central truth. Blind or otherwise, deluded about each other or not, Martin and Mary have found the love that springs from mutual need: perhaps, the play seems almost to suggest, the only love there is. But it is in the nature of the male to dream of conquest; and in that of the female to despise what she possesses on the grounds that it is less than all she might have had. Martin, restored to sight, finds only mockery and cruelty in the eyes of the girl who had seemed to encourage him. Mary in the end comforts herself with the thought that there are white-haired old women whom the young men never tire of looking at. But the last word is the Saint's; and although it appears to be about the old couple's choice of blindness, we are meant to feel the ironic implication, that it is about the emotional irrevocability of their choice of each other; 'They have chosen their lot, and the lord have mercy on their souls.'

The Well of the Saints abounds in ironies; in *The Playboy of the Western World* they are piled one on top of another in superb succession, and they are almost all related to what males have agreed among themselves to call the contrariness, the unpredictability, and the caprices of women. Never mind that the ultimate fraud is Christy, the greater crime, in the eyes of the ordinary male, is Pegeen's preference for him. The plot is too well known to need discussion: suffice it to say that neither Synge's preface, the anthropological school of criticism, the five hundred policemen, nor Yeats's idealizations of the peasantry can conceal the fact that the play is about the effect on women – on Pegeen Mike, the Widow Quin, and the famous drift of girls standing in their infamous shifts – of a man's fraudulent reputation for being a dangerous rogue; and that Pegeen Mike is one of the great feminine creations of dramatic literature, romantic, realist, obstinate, and tender all at once, while the Widow Quin is among the most memorable of women cynics. The fact that Christy, though a timid fraud, rises to great heights of daring and boldness while under the eyes of the girl he has beguiled is one of the ironies of the male's role, but the final master stroke concerns the woman's attitude, and it comes in the very last line. Pegeen has scorned and even hated him for the fraud he is discovered to be and the fool he has made of her, yet she cries out at the end: 'Oh my grief I've lost him surely. I've lost the only Playboy of the Western World.' He had, after all, the fine talk.

Deirdre of the Sorrows was written in the last year of Synge's life, when he probably knew he was dying, but when his relationship with Molly may have been, strangely enough, at its happiest. The usual misconceptions surround it. It is in no sense a classical tragedy (unless Conchubar, not Naisi, is the tragic hero) and the syntax is certainly not anglicized Irish. It is in fact, like all the others, a play about the unbiddability of the female heart, and its two highest moments are revelations of female psychology. One is Deirdre's reaction when she overhears her lover discussing with Fergus the possibility that they might grow tired of each other; the other is when, without hope of ever making amends, she reviles him for going off to die with his brothers and is immediately stricken by remorse for what can never be unsaid.

There are in fact few writers to equal this somewhat unsuccessful lover as an inventor of women and an observer of the situations they contrive to create out of what seems to male eyes mere caprice and wilfulness. That this 'ascendancy' writer succeeded in fashioning partly out of Irish syntactical modes and stored phrases a language to fit his own vision is part of his achievement, though it is largely fruitless to argue how much he owed to either memory or Irish. That he also decided to set his stories in the habitations of simple people where the mere sophistications of society would not occlude his vision or obscure their psychology we owe partly to his love for the bare and barren places of Ireland, but even more, in all probability, to the deep interior instincts of a great artist.

It would, on the face of it seem that the comic mis-conceptions inherent in the relationship of men and women appeal to Irish writers more than to others. Congreve, Sheridan, Wilde and Shaw, all more or less compatriots of Synge, had after all, been before him with the theme. But their interest had been as much in the societal misconceptions as in the psychological, the one sort admittedly feeding off the other, but the main burden of the comedy, with its societal archetypes, being in the interaction of the two. Synge sought out the primitive so that he could be free from these conventions and bring men and women face to face in a world where five pounds or a tin can were as important as a peerage or a great name. If, in doing so, he overlooked the strength of convention in his apparently primitive social milieux the fact is simply one further proof that he had, as an artist, a purpose other than the anthropological. That purpose was to expose the equivocations, the comic and tragic humiliations, 'the moods of varying rapture and dismay', the sheer bewilderment inherent in the relationships of men and women. It is done of course partly through male eyes: there would be no comedy if there were no dismayed or bewildered men. But whatever may be said about Wilde or Shaw, Synge is streets ahead of Congreve or Sheridan when it comes to understanding women and the springs of what the male merely sees as unpredictable and erratic behaviour. It is not, strangely enough, the successful lovers who know what Synge knew about women. And it is part of the triumph of the man as well as the artist that he feels with them, rejoices with them and laughs with them rather than with the almost always simpler, stupider and slower-witted males of his plays. Synge, the man, may have had a hard time of it with Molly; but he achieved as an artist the coolness of vision which is essential to comedy; and beneath all the comedy the underlying emotion is a veneration for the life-enhancing, convention-defying subtleties of feminine psychology which is rare enough in any literature; but which, taking Joyce and Yeats – not to mention Shaw – into account is, surprisingly or not, perhaps less rare in Irish literature than in some others.

Illustration 9: 'Selling on the Stones', St. Patrick's Street, before the market was closed by the Corporation in 1906. Synge Photo 18 (TCD)

9 | Bad At History
Anne Enright

> All of us know that Irishwomen are the most virtuous in the world.

It is a wonderful sentence. I thought it was said during the *Playboy* riots, I thought it was something to do with Pegeen in her shift, but in fact it was said in response to *The Shadow of the Glen* in 1903 and it was said by Arthur Griffith. I finally tracked it down to my school history text by F.S.L. Lyons, *Ireland since the Famine*. I have remembered this sentence for twenty-six years.

I have, in that time, forgotten who Arthur Griffith was, or I have remembered and forgotten again. Maybe I never really knew. When I look him up now I find that he was a member of the committee of the Irish National Theatre Society, along with Yeats and Lady Gregory. When *The Shadow of the Glen* was read in Lady Gregory's rooms in the Nassau Hotel, Maud Gonne and Douglas Hyde left the committee in a huff, while Griffith was prompted to set up his own organization, which he called Sinn Fein.

August 1903: this was the exact place where art and nationalist politics split. I wonder when it happened, and at what line. Perhaps it was when Nora told the tramp that she was not afraid of him, 'I never knew what way I'd be afeared of beggar or bishop or any man of you at all.' Maybe it was when she said, 'If it's a power of men I'm after knowing they were fine men, for I was a hard child to please, and a hard girl to please, and it's a hard woman I am to please this day.' Surely it was long before she gathered her fate about her, and chose the tramp, with, 'you've a fine bit of talk stranger and it's with yourself I will go.'

Whichever line it was, Nora Burke has a lot to answer for. She is the opposite of Cathleen ni Houlihan, the eponymous heroine of the play premiered in 1902, when the dramatic nationalists were all singing from the same hymn sheet and Maud Gonne enjoyed playing the role so much that it was with great difficulty she was persuaded to return the wig.

I am bad at history. Here are some facts: Arthur Griffith was initially in favour of a dual monarchy for Ireland and England. He once wrote an essay called 'The pirate, the freemason and the Jew.' No one told him about the Easter Rising, so he sat it out at home in Clontarf. He headed the Irish delegation negotiating the Treaty in London in 1921. In two years time I will have forgotten all these; the only thing I will remember about Arthur Griffith is that he's the stupid eejit who said, 'All of us know that Irishwomen are the most virtuous in the world.'

All of us? His Mammy knows it, and he knows it, and his sister knows it, and the boy on the butcher's bicycle knows it, and the tram conductor and the priest knows it, and the slavey knows it, and the second downstairs maid knows it, and they all go around knowing it all day long: because all of us (yes all of us!) know that the Phoenix Park is the largest enclosed park in Europe and O'Connell Street is the widest street in Europe and Irish women are the most virtuous in the world. More virtuous than Burkina Faso, certainly. Or Haute-Volta as it was then known.

Of these, the three founding myths of my Irish National School education - the park, the street and the lovely Irish girl, only one really endured. We were never much good, as a nation, at urban planning, but we did a mean job of keeping the lovely Irish girl lovely, for many decades to come.

Being bad at history, I go online to find out just who knew the thing about Irish women being the most virtuous in the world. A trawl at the more academic end of the internet yields three interesting returns for the phrase 'Irish prostitutes' (not that prostitutes are less virtuous than the rest of us – just that they are so clearly not the Rose of Tralee). The earliest, from 1776, comes from Adam Smith's 'The Wealth of Nations' where, as an economist, he is writing in praise of the potato as a staple food:

> The chairmen, porters, and coalheavers in London, and those unfortunate women who live by prostitution, the strongest men and the most beautiful women perhaps in the British dominions, are said to be the greater part of them from the lowest rank of people in Ireland, who are generally fed with this root.

Smith is quite casually of the opinion that prostitution was as Irish an activity as coalheaving. He does not say that these Irish women lack virtue, only that they are 'unfortunate'. He also thinks that they are beautiful. Smith may not think of the Irish as being separate in a modern sense; in this passage Irish merely seems to be of a piece with 'London poor'. So although he was not one of Griffith's 'all of us', this may have been before 'us' was invented. It is good to see at any rate that the lovely Irish girl, even in this early incarnation, was already considered lovely.

The second reference is to the nineteenth century scientist, George Cuvier who removed the reputedly super-sized genitals of Saartje Baartman, the 'Hottentot Venus', and put them in a jar for posterity. Writing about him, Elizabeth Alexander, Associate Professor at Yale, says:

> If you were to understand the essence of African women, he believed you should examine – indeed, dissect – their genitalia. He believed the same for Irish prostitutes.

It seems that Cuvier, a Frenchman, not only forgot what all of us know - namely, that Irishwomen are the most virtuous in the world – he went so far as to link them, anatomically, with a woman he considered to be halfway between mankind and the beasts.

The century that separates Smith and Cuvier saw a degradation of attitudes towards female sexuality – still, it is possible that two men will walk through a red light district, even today, and see very different women standing there. Whether Cuvier's problem was personal or historical, the sad fact of it is that when this man of science thought about Irish women he thought not of their poverty, their beauty, or their sad fate in life, but in a rigorously scientific way, of their nethers. Irish women, in this casual association with Saartje Baartman, were by anatomical imperative sexually depraved.

Cuvier met Baartman, naked and festooned with feathers, at a ball hosted by Madame du Barry: he dissected her body in 1815. The next reference to Irish prostitutes talks about the years after the famine. It is from an article by William J. Stern, who has written many times about the New York Irish in various respectable, if slightly right wing, publications:

> The Irish immigration of the 1840s was some 60 percent female, most of them single, and many of these newcomers soon found themselves on the street. Ronald H. Baylor and Timothy J. Meagher report in their book, *The New York Irish*, that the prostitute population jumped from 11,000 in 1839 to 50,000 ten years later, and these 'nymphs of the pave,' as people called them, were mostly young Irish girls. But it wasn't just prostitution: venereal disease, alcoholism, opium addiction, child abandonment, infanticide – the New York Irish suffered crippling levels of social pathology.

This figure of 50,000 Irish prostitutes on the streets of New York is so alarming that it deserves further investigation. Carol Groneman in the *Journal of Urban History*, looks at the incidence of prostitution in the immigrant Irish population and her abstract concludes that

> while family ties were strained by immigration, the Irish brought with them and maintained enduring family patterns and ways of life.

So Ms. Groneman might know it, but there are certainly many in the history game who are completely ignorant of the fact that Irish women are the most virtuous in the world. It seems that Arthur Griffith may have had very strong reasons for defending Irishwomen's honour: the poor and the displaced are often driven to prostitution; the 'racially inferior' are often considered to be sexually base. I want schoolchildren to be taught this, now, that the lovely Irish girl came from an Irish girl so poor she did not even own her body, and that is why we didn't allow contraception, abortion or divorce, or at least not on our native soil – because Irish women have always done bad things abroad, but *when they are at home* all of us know that Irish women are the most virtuous in the world.

In *A Portrait of the Artist*, Stephen Dedalus loses his virginity to a prostitute in a scene that is set around the turn of the century. When he first wanders into the red light district he wonders, in a disturbing echo of Griffith's anti-semitism, whether he has strayed into 'the quarter of the Jews'. It seems that, even for a writer as international and open as Joyce, there was something about all that sexual activity that was not strictly 'Irish.'

It is hard to say what Irish women were really like in 1903 – levels of prostitution may not be the best indicator; besides business was concentrated in urban areas (except for the Curragh) and the mythically pure Irishwoman was a country girl. Mind you, that other mythical Irishwoman, Griffith's fellow committee member on the Irish National Theatre Society, Maud Gonne, was not in the slightest bit virtuous. She conceived her second illegitimate child on the grave of her first, though Griffith was not to know that, or not that precisely, and besides the rules are always different for people like Maud Gonne, who was not, in the first instance, actually Irish.

It seems true to say that there was an increase in national virtuousness in the last years of the nineteenth century: there was, at any rate, a decline in the numbers of prostitutes. In her essay, 'Abandoned Women and Bad Characters: prostitution in nineteenth-century Ireland', Maria Luddy reports that the number of women arrested for offences other than soliciting in

1870 included 11,864 women thought to be prostitutes. That figure had declined to 2,970 by 1900. This she ascribes to the purity movement of the 1880s and also to the rise of a middle class morality among the survivors of the famine.

By the beginning of the twentieth century, many of the women admitted to the Magdalen homes were the 'seduced' daughters of the middle classes, rather than working prostitutes. After the withdrawal of British troops in 1922, business got even slower, and by 1925 the main brothels of Monto had been closed down. This was effected, in part, by the reforming zeal of the Legion of Mary, whose founder Frank Duff, estimated that there were 200 girls working there in 1922, and that, by 1925 this was reduced to 40. Underpinning his account of the fall of Monto, *Miracles on Tap*, is the sense that women themselves knew that they were out of joint with the times.

In July 1922, Duff took the first group of 23 'girls' off in a charabanc for a weekend retreat in Baldoyle, stopping briefly to pick up a Franciscan at Adam and Eve's church on the quays. He writes:

> As we go, we are brushing by history ... I bound creditably from my perch and run across the road to the door. If I had thought to look across the Liffey – as all those I left behind me were now doing, I would have witnessed a pitiful sight. Portions of the former proud walls of the Four Courts, the central law courts of Ireland, were being pulled down by great gangs of men with ropes. Civil War had just been raging, and these dangerously tottering walls were part of its grim heritage. And even during the short time I was away, our great adventure was in peril: the result of that striking scene playing upon supercharged nerves and galvanizing into life that old terror to which reference has already been made, that a government plot was in operation against them. What were those soldiers stalking about with rifles for and looking – many of them – in the direction of the vivid-coloured charabanc? Did they not look as if they were going to shoot at it?

Fatefully, by Frank Duff's account, the charabanc did not contain Honour Bright, who changed her mind at the last minute because she 'did not want to leave her baby', and was subsequently killed, while working, in 1926. Testimony at her murder trial shows that although Monto was quiet, business was still brisk outside the Shelbourne, where girls and jarveys provided a 'once around the Green' service for gentlemen at the end of their evening. Accounts of the trial, as well as interviews with former residents of Monto, make it clear that the Dublin poor had a great sympathy for the 'unfortunate girls' working in their midst, and that many of the better-off were equally slow to judge. When Arthur Griffith talked about 'all of us' he was conjuring a middle class that did not yet exist; this was the same 'nearly' middle class that Synge abhorred, perhaps because he was looking at it from the other side.

> The groggy-patriot-publican-general-shop-man who is married to the priest's half-sister and is second cousin once-removed of the dispensary doctor ... are horrible and awful.

Synge wishes he could put these people on stage. 'God, wouldn't they hop!' In his letter to a friend about his travels in the West, he is distressed to find,

> in one place the people are starving but wonderfully attractive and charming, and in another place where things are going well, one has a rampant, double-chinned vulgarity I haven't seen the like of.

Arthur Griffith may be a prime example of this 'rampant double-chinned vulgarity', but perhaps he had a stronger idea than Synge of what it was to be poor (but wonderfully attractive), and on the boat, and on your back. Besides, how was he to know that polemic always fades, while art survives?

On the opening night of *The Shadow of the Glen*, Yeats, in what an onlooker described as 'his usual thumpty thigh, monotonous, preachy style', stood up in the Molesworth Hall and 'defended the artist's right to show life, instead of the desire which every political party would substitute for life.' His spat with Griffith rose to a pitch with the *Playboy* in 1907, which Griffith described as

> a vile and inhuman story told in the foulest language we have ever listened to from a public platform ... the production of a moral degenerate, who has dishonoured the women of Ireland before all Europe.

In the characters of Nora Burke, Pegeen Mike and the
Widow Quin, Synge was drawing on a pre-famine tradition of
women who are strong, and likeable, and free enough. The
lovely Irish girl had too much mischief in her ever to be really
good, and all through the twentieth century Synge's characters
gave the lie to the legislative piety of Griffith's inheritors. You
could say that the war goes on, though the most convincing
battles were fought in the referendums of the 1980s.

Now, from a tired distance of twenty years, it seems to me
that this second Irish Civil War, the one we fought about
contraception, abortion and divorce, wasn't actually about
virtue – or only incidentally so – it was about breeding. It was
about maintaining stock. The country faced a demographic shift
towards the young. We could not believe that, for the first time
since the famine, the population of Ireland did not have to
overproduce just to keep still.

I grew up during the 1980s. For very good reasons, I am bad
at history. Much better, like Synge, to stick to art.

One last thing: through all the hard years of the twentieth
century, Pegeen Mike ran around in her shift on stages all over
Ireland, both amateur and professional. She has a lot to answer
for. There hasn't been an Irish production since without a
woman in her shift, or 'slip', as they are now known. Forget the
pan of rashers, it is the woman standing in her slip with a
regretful look on her face that marks the Abbey production out
for me. 'Run out there to Guiney's and get me another twenty
mixed slips,' says the Wardrobe Mistress to the Assistant
Wardrobe Mistress, 'These ones are getting a bit yellow under
the arms.'

A woman in her slip, I think it is fair to say, is someone who
has just had sex with the main character. She is not married,
because a married woman on an Irish stage would always wear a
dressing gown. The woman in the slip reads as 'naked', though
this is complicated by the fact that the actress wearing the slip
also wears various other undergarments, even when sitting up,
post-coitally, in bed. This is in case her nipples might show.

Pegeen, in her Ur-slip, had a better time than any of them,
and this I take as a sign that Synge was a better writer of

women than those who came after him. The first are often the best. In *Riders to the Sea* he instituted another great trope of the Irish Theatre – the dead child. This is a child that the audience has never seen, heard, or met, who dies offstage to leave its mother grieving for the duration. Maurya, the mother in the play, has six of them, which makes her a hard act to follow. Synge may have thought he was being Greek about this, but subsequent playwrights just think they are being Irish. They seem to think that if a woman says, 'I had a child and it died' we will always believe them, in a way that we do not believe a dead body on stage: in the way, indeed, in which we do not believe a child onstage.

I only mention this because off-stage dead children always make me cry, and after many years of crying in precisely the same way for different dead children I realize that it is always the same child that is on my mind, and he (it is always a boy) is always blonde and curly-haired and about six years old. I don't know why, it is just that when a woman, often in her slip, touches her belly and talks about the child she had that died, or the child she nearly had, that died, I feel a caption should scroll across the top of the proscenium arch saying, *Women have their sadness too*. Though it is possible that these male playwrights are saying that a woman's sadness is the only sadness; there is no other kind, and all the rest is noise.

Illustration 10: Molly Allgood. TCD 6198/14

10 | Collaborators

By Joseph O'Connor

There is a part of the garden, by the cluster of sycamores, near the bend in the drive where the gravel is wearing thin. If he stands there, quietly, on a still Sunday morning, when none of the servants is around to annoy him, and when Mother is up in her room at her scriptures, he can hear the distant approach of the train from Dublin: the windborne shush-and-chug that means she might be coming to him again. He is thirty-six now, already very ill. Painful years have passed since he stopped believing he could be loved. The power of what is happening terrifies him.

He leaves his mother's garden, makes hurriedly for Glenageary station: up the willow-lined avenue, towards St Paul's, Church of Ireland. Past the entrance to the quarry-lanes known locally as 'The Metals', through which the granites were hefted long ago for the stanchions of Kingstown Pier. There are days when he feels hammered; his breathing sometimes knifes him. But punctuality is important, a sign of respect.

The walk from his mother's house takes about seven minutes. Often, he arrives as the locomotive is chuntering to its screechy standstill and belching grimy spumes of cinders and mizzle. He skulks in the station portico, not daring to hope, lowering his eyes quickly if a neighbour happens past. It would not do to be seen: not yet, not here. There is the age-difference between them. There are other differences, too.

And then – where can she be? – she materializes through the smoke. There she is, beckoning circumspectly from a Second-Class window. It is like a small moment out of Tolstoy, perhaps, one of those seemingly simple but reverberating images he values in the novels of Russia. He pictures her stepping down through the vapour, the soot, and then hurrying along the platform to him, parasol in hand. She comes to him through the filth, her face hopeful and kind, the steam moistening a strand of hair to her forehead. But this can not happen. People might see. There would be talk around Glenageary.

Instead he boards the train, takes the bench opposite her in the carriage. They are like a couple of collaborators plotting a treason. Outside, the conductor is slamming the doors. A whistle is blown. A green flag is flourished. As the engine gives a shriek and they judder away from Glenageary, he begins to feel something like relief.

From the pocket of her raincoat is protruding a playscript, he notices. She uses the journey to learn her lines. No one could say she is beautiful, exactly, but she is an actress: she is able to decide whether to be beautiful or plain. Like a 'changeling,' he tells her; his preferred endearment: like many sweet nothings, an ambiguity.

The train clatters into the tunnel at Killiney. He is alone with her in darkness. He feels her hand steal into his. This thrills him, charges him. *No one can see.* The moment passes quickly, there is a sudden dazzle of light, and the panorama of the bay is magnificent: Italian. It will not be too long more before they come coasting into Bray, where nobody knows him. Bray is safe.

Passers-by might think them a father and daughter, as they exit Bray station, and she links him at the elbow, and they go walking down the promenade in the direction of the Head, through a swirl of dirty gulls and old newspapers. He looks older than his years; she looks younger than hers. He has achieved some recognition in the field of playwriting – translations of two of his works have been performed in Prague and Berlin, he is co-director of the Irish National Theatre

Society – but few in this frumpy Little Brighton would know he was a writer, and fewer, if they did, would care. His companion has appeared in three of his plays: bit parts at first, but she was soon elevated to leads.

Their affair is a year old. He has been hurt in love previously, has long been introspective, harrowed by depressions. Social life in Dublin he finds a crucifixion. He loathes the vulgarity, the backslappery and falseness: 'the cheap commonplace merriment' of it all. He tells her she should be civil to her fellow actors – 'steadily polite' is the way he puts it – but must always wear a mask, must never trust outsiders. (By 'outsiders' he means everyone except himself.) Above all, their engagement is to remain a secret. There could be whisperings in the theatre. People would have views. Yeats and Lady Gregory do not think it quite correct for a co-director and a mere actress to be so familiar. There is also the problem of Mother, of course. The news will have to be broken very gradually to Mother.

They slog around Bray, back to Loughlinstown, or Shankill, trudging weedy rutted laneways, puddled boreens, like a schoolboy and his first sweetheart on a glum little tryst with no money to go in someplace out of the rain. The things he finds fascinating, she can't understand them. Rocks. Bushes. Moths. Deserted nests. A squirrel – look! – falling out of a tree! ('Holy Moses,' yelps the playwright: his favourite profanity.) This dreamer is a covey who gazes into a hedgerow like a debutante staring into a jeweller's window.

She does not like all this walking, becomes tired very quickly. Unlike her Old Tramp – this is how he styles himself – she has to work hard, whether or not she is sick. There are no housemaids, no servants in the place she calls home. She rehearses most days, is on the stage almost nightly. She has not yet fully learned the breathing techniques of an actor, that acting is about the body as much as the instincts, and the director is pushing her hard. The work is demanding, often exhausting. So she sees walking as primarily a means of getting to some destination, whereas Mister Honey appears to regard it as an end in itself. Occasionally she suspects he feels the same way about courtship. An agreeable hobby, not leading to anything but literature.

He feels strongly that she should learn, should improve her mind. It is time for her to stop reading 'dressmaker's trash.' He gives her novels he has selected, volumes of verse. Soon she will be 'the best-educated actress in Europe,' he says, as though the phrase might one day appear on a poster bearing her image. He wants her to take pride in what he calls her progress. She is to keep notebooks of her reading, as he does of his own, listing works for which she cares and the reasons why. He has 'wheelbarrow-loads' of such jotters at home in Glenageary. He has been keeping them for years. She should acquire this practice. There is a touch of Pygmalion and the Statue in what is happening between them, but there are times when she wonders which of them is which.

'Come down and learn to love and be alive.' In the version by William Morris, whose work he admires, this is the plea of unhappy Pygmalion to the cold marble effigy he so agonizingly loves. She wonders if her playwright, her lover of stones, has ever given thought to this supplication, how he would respond if he found himself its recipient.

He drifts, this tweedy tramp, dusty gentleman of the roads. Kilmacanogue. Enniskerry. The dolmens of Ballybrack. The backwoods and cart-tracks of the Dublin-Wicklow borderlands. He has no map, no compass, no plan except to keep walking. Over the crest of the next hummock, there will always be another one. Around lakes. Into grottoes. Through forests. Across streams. Jesus, can he walk. He must be the healthiest invalid in Ireland. No holy well or hermitage is allowed to remain unpoked-at. They traipse up and down the Sugarloaf until she can tell all the sheep apart. A pity love is not measured in worn-out soles; if it were, she would be a married woman by now.

Several times they have agreed on a date for their wedding. Always he finds a reason for the plan to be deferred. As a student, a capable violinist, he gave up the ambition of professional musicianship, because the petrifaction of stage-fright was too much for him to face. He is still frozen in the wings, she sometimes thinks, afraid to step out into the scene that is begging for him.

Probably some of this is Mother's doing. His childhood was one of 'well-meant but extraordinary cruelty.' She gruelled him on the bible, on the castigations of Hell. He has been slowly roasted on the flames of her widowhood. He could never be a father, he resolved while still a child; parents bequeath us only their susceptibilities. 'I will never create beings to suffer as I am suffering.' She has an image of a terrified newborn, croop-racked, asthmatic, flailing at the banshees that swoop at his cot.

He doesn't belong. Doesn't want to belong. That isn't quite right: he wants *not* to belong. 'I am always a kind of outsider,' he claims, yet he never stops fretting about what people will think. Life is drearily hateful in the bourgeois suburbs: 'Kingstown, the heat, and the frowsy women.' But it is to here he returns at the end of the day, when the rambles are over and the house-lights fade back up. His changeling is left to rehearse unspoken lines on a train to an empty room in the city.

Should they happen to see one another in the theatre during the week, he does not like them to converse. People might be listening. 'You must not mind,' he tells her, 'if I seem a little distant. We can have our talk on green hills, that are better than all the green rooms in the world.' Her mother, various friends all caution her to be careful, but she won't be said: they don't understand. She is only nineteen, she knows this is love. What matter if he's a little odd? Writers often are.

Sunday is their usual day; she takes the quarter-to-eleven from Tara Street. It is a standing arrangement, but he often reminds her of it by letter. They roam the furzy slopes of Killiney Hill, or lie among its alpines looking down at the bay. The setting has the dual advantage of being Wordsworthian and discreet. Here they can be alone, almost certain of privacy. They feed one another the wild berries that grow near the obelisk: '*fraughans*' in the vernacular, but she calls them 'purple grapes'. This becomes one of their euphemisms, a love-phrase charged with intimate meaning. The fairy-woman and the vagabond, their transgressive liaison. It is like a scene from a folktale, the seed of one of his plays. Who is emancipating whom?

Sometimes he recites the lyrics he has written for her: his gifts. 'I wrote another poem on you last night,' he confides, as though he had somehow imprinted it on her flesh. But these verses are rarely sensual, are often a little oblique. Only seldom does he tell her, very shyly, like a boy, how much he likes to see her 'in light summer clothes.' At such moments, strangely, she has a powerful sense of his brokenness, of how difficult he finds it just being alive. There are days when he looks at an oak and sees only the makings of a coffin. He has no memory of his father, who died when he was a baby.

He can be jealous, furiously so, if he senses a rival in the picture. She is not to talk to other men, not to take one by the arm, is never to offer anything that might be read as an encouragement. Medical students, especially, are to be shunned, he insists. Such oafs are debauchers who 'dangle out of actresses' and brag of their seductions, of innocents led on. He is not himself a dangler, a stage-door Johnnie. No gentleman would inveigle a girl by holding out false hopes.

He is not conventionally handsome; that goatee makes him appear shifty. A face like a blacking brush, as one of his friends puts it. He looks faintly like a typical Irishman in an old Punch cartoon: beetle-browed, mercurial, recently down from the trees. But he is not a typical Irishman: he loves to listen. His few true confidantes have all been women. ('People like Yeats who sneer at old fashioned goodness and steadiness in women seem to want to rob the world of what is most sacred in it.') She talks to him about her clothes, about hats and gowns, her difficult sister, problems with money, arguments at rehearsal, ghastly 'digs' she has stayed in, grim tours around the provinces, her painful menstruations. He arranges for her to attend an eminent gynaecologist in Dublin; cannot bear the thought that she would be in needless pain. She used to be a shopgirl: she tells him about that. She smokes, quite heavily, and he nags at her to stop it.

He relishes the simple intimacies; of this she is certain. No man she has known has craved them more. And yet, when they holiday one weekend in the hills, he is adamant that they must take separate cottages. She finds him so queer. He is 'highly-strung,' he informs her. Every writer is. This is the price of art. She knows the price of art, has been paying it for some time. Some of the love-poems she has inspired seem like howls of grief.

He talks to her about Paris, about Germany and the Aran Islands, where the people are serious and allow you to be alone among them. He longs to show her these places. When they are married, he will. Everything will be all right when they marry, he feels, though Mother often wonders, as he can't help but do himself, how he and a wife could manage on a writer's pittance. (This is Mother's way of making it clear that the family silver will not be subsidizing love-in-a-garret.) He hungers for the success that can give them independence. To escape from Glenageary, to make his own way: the need comes to fume in him like a lust.

He is working on a strange piece, set in a kind of Lilliputian Mayo, about a storyteller who bludgeons his father and becomes a hero in the process. The play is sending him mad; the correct shape for it is eluding him. He has been trying to conceal structural weakness with what he calls 'strong writing', but is beginning to discern that this is a cheat, that form and content must be wedded more tightly. He thinks there is a great role in it for his changeling, perhaps. His 'Pigeen', as he has taken to calling her lately.

They talk about this role. He listens while she talks. She is adaptable, amenable. Which changeling is not? She thinks he is a genius. He tells her that *she* is. She loves his dedication, his monkish graveness. Beside him, even severe old Augusta Gregory can seem a high-kicker auditioning for a cabaret. He talks about his characters as though they were real. 'I wrestle with that playboy,' he jokes bleakly, but he means it. It is as though these voluble buckos and fiery-tongued colleens were to be encountered any evening on a stroll through Mother's garden.

He reads her a few soliloquies of the play set in Mayo, one warm Sunday evening on Killiney Hill. A bachelor is a ridiculous figure, he recites, 'like an old braying jackass strayed upon the rocks.' He looks up at her hopefully. Is that right, he wonders?

It is whispered among the stagehands that his people are landlords down the country, that they evicted tenants in the bad times, burned their cabins. Many's the tramp has been created by this family, relatively few of them fictional. She gathers that he quarrelled with Mother about the evictions, but Mother pointed out, evidently with scriptural vehemence, that the tenants down the country were paying for his freedom to write, so he was hardly in a position to be adopting revolutionary poses. Mother and her sister grew up on the neighbouring estate to the Parnells', often rocked his little cradle when the Chief was a baby. In later years, Aunt Jane grew fond of remarking what a pity it was that they didn't take the opportunity to strangle him.

Months turn to seasons. Rehearsals turn to shows. His eyes are darkening; the weather she sees in them is sullen. He seems half in love with death, like Keats watching nightingales. Christmases come and go, and he coughs like a broken train, and still the old lady refuses to die. He is nearly always sick now: the growth on his neck makes him quake. There are fears he might be tubercular. He may need aggressive surgery. Often, he takes to his bed for days. He becomes convinced that the effort of writing 'brings fever.'

And there is trouble at the theatre; there are faction fights, rows. What is it in theatre people that must always squabble? He is not a committeeman like Yeats, or a battler like Her Ladyship, though he is conscientious about management, thinks it important. But he'd rather be in Wicklow, roaming his rocks, 'away from all good commonplace people,' he says. He starts to advise his changeling to become a writer herself. She is already a writer; she just doesn't know it.

They write to each other daily, sometimes twice in the space of a morning. The reason, he says, is that she is never far from his thoughts. Often, while he is headlocking the playboy in Glenageary, or bicycling the dappled avenues, which he likes to do at dusk, when everything is quiet and he can breathe a little easier, she drifts onto the stage of his mind. He loves her so fiercely; he won't let anyone hurt her, ever. 'Not even yourself,' he can't help but add. His true nature is so kind, so scrupulously gentle; but always he feels the need to cloak it in ironies. He is the sad kind of Irishman who seems embarrassed by his own decency. 'An afflicted poor devil,' as he sometimes says.

She feels, if they courted more often and openly, that there would be less of a need for letters, and that this would be a relief. He rarely stops chiding her for not writing to him often enough. She doesn't say what she means, she writes too briefly, she forgets about his illnesses, she breaks all her promises, she wants too much from him, she doesn't want enough, she looked at him coldly, she winked at some spear-carrier. A Kingstown postmark makes her feel trepidation; the way his mother would feel if she glanced up from Leviticus and saw a tricolour flapping from the conservatory roof. If only they could spend time actually having their feelings, rather than thinking up new ways of putting them into words. But he seems to think nothing is real unless it is written down. (The heroine of his Mayo play will be first encountered writing a letter.)

She has noticed that 'lonesome' is the adjective he most uses about himself. He is nearly always lonesome in his missives to his changeling. Another word he likes to deploy is 'disappointed'. It is sprinkled over his letters like a tartish cologne. She disappoints him so often, so deeply and unforgivably, that there are times when she can't help but wonder what he is doing with her at all.

He often repeats a story she has always found curious, emblematic of him in some way neither of them quite understands: about a particular sojourn he once made into Wicklow, when the room in which he quartered was directly above a kitchen, so that if he got down on the floorboards and put his ear to the chinks, he could eavesdrop on the serving girls talking below him. An admirer of Shakespeare, perhaps he thought of Pyramus and Thisbe, those lovers doomed to commune through a fissure in a wall. Maybe – can this be possible? – he sees her as a conduit, a way of negotiating away that separation? It is easier for a camel to go through the eye of a needle than for a Kingstowner to navigate that eye in the floor. She is the only woman of her class with whom he has ever been truly intimate, perhaps the only Irish catholic who will ever know him really well. (Unless some gurleen over in Aran? – but no. He'd be afraid.) Is her role to be conductress, to allow him *admission* to something? 'Be careful not to get grease-paint in your eyes,' he once told her. Be careful yourself, she sometimes wants to say. The twilight is not real; it is only limelight burning low. So much in the theatre is smoke and mirrors.

Like many self-doubting people, he sometimes has the arrogance of a Pharaoh. She has received love letters before, but never like his. Who in the name of the suffering saints does this thread-arsed playmaker think he is? The proper mode of such correspondence, when written by men, is to pronounce oneself unworthy of the fairy-one's favours, to do a little begging and gasping about your sleeplessness, and make a few suggestive comparisons to mythological hip-swingers. It doesn't matter that you don't mean it: Christ, it's only good form. But the playboy doesn't play. These are not *billets-doux*.

He tells her, approvingly, that she is 'pretty and quiet and nice.' Is that really what he burns for in a lover, she wonders, and is this sandwich of stone-like, deadly words the best way a poet would have of presenting it? Why does he never say exactly what he wants? Would that be too much to ask, too naked an admission? If beauties were before me, stepping out of their clothes, it would be you that I'd beg for; it could only be you. Why can he never write her anything like that?

Mostly, his tone is sardonic, schoolmasterly; so brusque he seems to want to push her away. 'I will not wait for you in Bray, so don't miss your train.' 'I'm afraid I'm spoiling you by writing to you every day.' 'You may be sure when I have anything I don't approve of, I'll let you know fast enough.' 'Why are you so changeable when you know how much it hurts and harms me?' He is an example of the man every woman has known: the suitor who craves you but secretly wants to be dismissed.

Their quarrels are Vesuvian tirades of invective. 'You are ludicrous!' she accuses him. 'You may stop your letters if you like. I don't care if I never heard from you or saw you again, so there!' She is faithless, he is 'selfpitiful', she is spiteful, he is 'an old stick in the mud'. They can have no possible future, should separate immediately. She is making him ill. He is wearing her out. She will leave off acting and 'get a shop' if he keeps this up. (That will soften his cough for him now.) One of her outbursts is countered by Glenageary's ultimate denunciation: 'You have finally *ruined* my holiday.'

He loves to take his seat in the consoling darkness of the theatre, to watch her move about in the scorch of the light: the poise with which she holds herself, the way she speaks his lines. The fact of her speaking them, a kind of lovemaking.

She moves across the footlights, knowing he is watching. Up here, she is the artist, he the apprentice. He is out beyond the point where anything matters. Not riots. Not hypocrisies. Not batons. Nothing. *'That is not the West!'* a man in the audience cries out, as though he were in the play, which, in a way, he is; he will always be in it now, no matter where or in what circumstances it is ever performed again. And she feels for this man. She understands his grief. All those years he was told that his West was a land of apes. He wants it to be a land of angels, is upset and frightened that it isn't. But she clings to the lines. People are yelling. As the cries grow more wounded, and the insults crueller, she pictures her lover silently mouthing his lines along with her. She feels like weeping, but that will not happen. She breathes and speaks, she speaks and breathes, and the words he wrote in silence are pushed into the air. Acting is breathing: the body gives life. Some reason, a small one, but it isn't nothing, to go on existing in this vicious world, where hurts abound, and the body fails, and the crushed hopes of childhood are never far away. It is an act of mercy, the thing she does every night. She would be nothing without him. He needs her, too.

They are walking up Bray Head, as they often do on Sundays, and below them the sea is a rolling grey-green. People are nudging. They know him now. The Kingstown little tinker who wrote that dirty play. He does not seem put out, nor even especially surprised. 'We are an event,' he tells her, and they carry on with the climb. Pushing together into the slab of the gradient. It is as though he is trying to persuade himself that none of it matters. 'It makes me rage when I think of the people who go on as if art and literature and writing were the first thing in the world.' He is so disingenuous sometimes. You'd have to love him.

Soon he will alter his term of address. 'My child,' he will call her, instead of 'my changeling.' He is aging with every step, is often in crippling pain. 'I am so proud of you,' he says. 'I am so fond of you. I love you.'

Before very long, his mother will die, so old that he doesn't remember her age any more. His loyalty to her ghost is unqualified, fervent. It is as though she is still in the house, watching over his shoulder, still waiting for him to atone for all the disappointments. 'I cannot tell you how unspeakably sacred her memory seems to me,' he will write. 'There is nothing in the world better or nobler than a single-hearted wife and mother. I wish you had known her better. I hope you'll be as good to me as she was.' How hard it must have been to write such words. But harder to have had to read them.

He will stay on in the big house at Glenageary for a time, but will find it difficult to be alone in the old empty rooms, with only 'that little donkey of a servant' for company. He will inherit some money, not very much, but enough to live quietly in some place like Dundrum. That is all he wants now: his child and Dundrum. A home with no memories. A few quiet years together. He is becoming like Lear, as the play nears its end: begging for the consolations he refused in Act One. Being killed by the Gods for their sport.

He will talk to her again about marriage, their future. 'If only my health holds we will be able to get on now.' But the cues have all been missed; he did not recognize them when they came, and the long-rehearsed plans are not to be realized. Five painful months after the death of his mother, he himself will die, aged thirty-eight, following a hopeless operation for Hodgkin's disease. Distraught, she will beseech a priest to say a requiem mass, but will be told that the request is difficult to grant. He was not one of us. He was of the other persuasion. There have to be limits, after all.

Probably he would have understood, would not have wanted any fuss. All his life he had to attune to subtle transmissions of his unacceptability. He knew what it is to find yourself walled out, separated by boundaries you did not yourself make; to have to look through whatever chink may be found at the people whose acknowledgement you ached for. At the time of his death, no member of his family has ever seen one of his plays.

'My dearest Love,' begins his farewell letter. 'This is a mere line for you, my poor child, to bid you good-bye and ask you to be brave and good and not to forget the good times we've had and the beautiful things we've seen together.'

It is signed 'Your old Friend.' He is no longer the tramp. There is no need to be in character any more.

She will help Yeats and Lady Gregory to stitch together his last play, will continue at acting, will emigrate to London. She will be married twice, will give birth to two children, will often be close to poverty, will not always be happy. She will never give up, will always act; but as she ages there will be years when living gets very much harder. She begins to drink heavily; her private life is troubled; her son, an RAF man, is killed during the war. There are not many parts for an elderly Irish actress in England, whose great performances are over and whose manner can be difficult. *The good times we've had and the beautiful things we've seen.* He was right: it takes bravery to remember such times. Bravery and goodness. The ultimate defiance.

Molly Allgood, whose stage-name was Maire O'Neill, will die in London, in the winter of 1952, having collapsed while rehearsing a radio play.

Her daughter is 'Pegeen' after her mother's greatest role: a woman who loves a storyteller, but loses him too soon, when the past lurches out from the dark backstage in the shape of his wounded parent.

'All art is a collaboration,' wrote the father of the play.

'To me, he was everything,' said the mother.

Illustration 11: Aaron Monaghan in the DruidSynge production of *The Playboy of the Western World* (2005). Photograph by Toni Wilkinson

11 | Wild And Perfect: Teaching
The Playboy of the Western World
Roddy Doyle

The best thing about *The Playboy of the Western World* is the
voices. The thing is full of culchies. It's a teacher's dream.
Try finding enough students willing to read the parts in Hamlet.
'Hands up who wants to be Laertes.'
Hands stay down; eyes hit the desk. You're standing in front of
a roomful of very shy, aspiring vets and accountants. Not an
actor or a chancer among them.
But come back in six months with *The Playboy*.
'Hands up who wants to be Shawn Keogh.'
'Sir!'
'Sir!'
'Me sir!'
'Sir!'
'Me, me, me, me, me!'
'What about the Widow Quinn?'
'Oh God, pick me!'

I was an English teacher for fourteen years. I spent hours,
days, months trying to convince young people that the irony in
Persuasion was worth their attention. 'There's a good laugh on
the next page; I swear.'

I spent hours and days trying to convince them that
Wordsworth wasn't an eejit. 'They're only flowers, Sir. Calm
down.'

That Yeats wasn't an eejit – 'Sir? Why didn't he just ask her to go with him?'; that every sentence and line they read wasn't, automatically, the work of an eejit.

It was a constant fight. I stood at the front of the room and said, 'Open up _____' (Choose any one of the following: *Persuasion*, *The Charwoman's Daughter*, *Heartbreak House*, most of the pages in *Soundings*, *Portrait of a Lady*, *The Greatest of These* – and the list goes on. The horror!)

The command to open the text was always followed by a groan. A real groan. The dreadful, wet sound of young minds being squeezed. I was killing these children. But there were plenty of good days. The students were easily convinced that Shakespeare was the business. They loved Edmund. They loved Lady Macbeth. They loved Iago. They loved *Wuthering Heights*. They loved Heathcliff and Cathy. They loved hating the other characters. They loved the passion and the cruelty. They loved *Lord of the Flies*. They loved Piggy, and the 'stuff' coming out of his head. They loved the posh English boys shoving, hitting – killing each other. 'Sucks to your asthmarr!'

They loved the fact that these kids could have been themselves; they loved the honesty of the book, the language, and the simplicity of the story – the theme: children, given the chance and the island, will eat one another. And they loved – God, they loved – *The Playboy of the Western World*.

'Sir!'

'Sir!'

'Me!'

It was, at first, the opportunity to do the voices. The room was suddenly full of Christys and Pegeen Mikes. Even the girl I chose to read the stage instructions became a culchie, an R.T.E. continuity announcer circa 1981. 'Impty barrels stind near di counter.'

It was mad, wild stuff. A laugh. These Dublin kids got it out of their systems. Every Garda who'd ever told them to move their arses, every teacher who'd ever looked sideways at them, every priest who'd ever let his Mass go over the thirty-five minutes – they all got a slagging in the first few pages of *The Playboy*.

'Where's himself?'

Shawn Keogh, 'a fet ind fair young min', is the first male character to walk onstage. In the first few days of reading, Shawn came from Kerry, Donegal, Galway, Offaly, Limerick, Wexford and, bizarrely, Scotland. One boy in the class could do a good Sean Connery and decided not to waste it.

'Where'sh himshelf?'

James Bond had just walked into the shebeen, but Pegeen Mike didn't even look up. If I remember correctly – and I probably don't – the first Pegeen Mike, having beaten off the opposition, decided to stick with her own accent. So, for the first five or six pages, Pegeen Mike Flaherty, 'a wild-looking but fine girl', came from Briarfield Grove, Kilbarrack, two minutes walk from the Dart station.

'Isn't ih long the nights are now, Shawn Keogh, to be leavin' a poor girl wi'h her own self countin' the hours to the dawn o' day?'

James Bond's response was lost in the roars and wolf-whistles.

It was fun, but not much else, at first. The first few pages were very slow. Pegeen's shopping list on the first page seemed unnecessarily verbose, and we were expected to watch her write it. And what did those words mean? 'A hat is suited for a wedding day.' Did she want a hat? And what was a hat doing on a shopping list? Where were the eggs and the bread? And why all the names on the first two pages? Philly Cullen and Red Linahan, the mad Mulrannies and Father Reilly, Marcus Quinn, 'got six months for maiming ewes'. It was one line, stop, next line, stop, just like reading Shakespeare for the first time, until they got the hang of it, until they could see it, and hear it, and it began to make great sense.

It did make great sense. And, along the way, it was often hilarious. One of the great successes of my career in teaching came to me unexpectedly, when Shawn Keogh delivered the line, 'I'm after feeling a kind of fellow above in the furzy ditch'. The Shawn that morning was from somewhere near Kerry, but his accent fell away when he got to 'fellow' and he realized what he'd just read, and the other twenty-nine boys and girls in the

room realized what he'd just read, and the silence – it lasted less
than a second - became a cheer that became a bigger cheer, and
bigger, and Shawn Keogh looked at his desk, and under his
desk, for the hole he hoped would swallow him whole, and
burp. And, after the laughter died and Shawn Keogh
rediscovered his spine, I never before saw such keen
scholarship; every student was flying through the pages, looking
for more lines like that one. I hoped the principal or vice-
principal would walk in now; I hoped anyone would walk in. I
was listening to the sound of utter concentration. I had control
and engagement. And I had silence. No threat or bribe would
ever again be as effective. And I had it, the sound of well-used
silence – it's very, very rare – for two long minutes, until
someone found Shawn Keogh's line about 'the naked parish'.

'What page, what page?'– and that started another scramble.

Then someone else found the Widow Quin talking about
'the gallant hairy fellows are drifting beyond', and that got me
up to the bell and the coffee break. I bought myself a Twix.
At first, the language of *The Playboy* was as far away from these
Dublin kids as the language of Chaucer and Shakespeare. Even
the simple question from the Widow Quin, 'What kind was he?'
needed a good looking at before it became, 'What was he like?'
or something nearer their words. 'There's harvest hundreds do
be passing these days for the Sligo boat.' Again, it needed
staring at. What was a 'curiosity man'? And what did 'Tuesday
was a week' mean? But, as with Shakespeare, the staring was
well worth the time. 'Harvest hundreds' brought a story about
one girl's grandfather who went from Donegal to Scotland
every year to pick potatoes. And, more than twenty years later, I
still meet ex-students who smile and say, 'Tuesday was a week'.

The Playboy was a hit. It wasn't just because they could
become culchies for the day. They copped on to the story and,
unlike the language, the story was immediately theirs. I taught
The Playboy in the early '80s, when many of these kids were
going to join the 'harvest hundreds'. The play was about people
on the edge of the rules, and the kids I taught knew that place.
Today, that part of north Dublin is often featured in the
Property sections – the schools, the sea, all the recently

discovered amenities. Back then, it looked much as it does now but, more than once, I saw the word 'ghetto' used to describe it. It was no more a ghetto than Ranelagh, but these kids knew the hurt of being written off. They knew the power and fun of language; language was one of the things they owned. Slagging was a sport and an art. The best slag I heard was this: 'Your granny'd climb out of her grave for a half-bottle of gin.' Change it a bit and it could be a line from *The Playboy*; it might even have been in the first draft. It's a *Playboy* line because *The Playboy* is a slagging play. The slags fly across and back across the stage. Pegeen Mike and the Widow Quin, the big women of the play, are particularly good at it – 'there's poetry talk for a girl you'd see itching and scratching'. Slagging is a huge part of the play's energy. Shakespeare knew a well-aimed slag. So did Synge. And so did my students.

And they knew a great story. 'Tell us a film' I'd ask one particular student when I was feeling lazy, and he'd stand up and deliver the plot of whatever video he'd watched the night before. I'd seen some of the films; he was much, much better. Is wasn't just entertainment. I could see that on his face, and I could see it in the faces of the others watching and listening. It was vital; it was power. He had them. These minutes might have been the highpoint of his life. It's not just the plot of *The Playboy*. It's the man in the middle, Christy, telling the story, making himself up, assembling himself with words. I don't know what age he's supposed to be, what age Synge had in mind when he made him cough offstage, before he walks on, 'a slight young man … very tired and frightened and dirty'. He's a teenager. (So is Pegeen Mike.) He's lost and he's shy. But he talks; he makes up his story. He's listened to, and he has power.

Then there's Christy's story. ' … wasn't I a foolish fellow not to kill my father in the years gone by.' Sophocles only had it half-right. No true Irish boy wants to sleep with his mother. But killing the Da is a different proposition. 'I just riz the loy', says Christy, 'and let fall the edge of it on the ridge of his skull.' Once they knew that a 'loy' was kind of a shovel and that 'riz' meant lifting it over his Da's head, all faces in the room lit up. These were teenagers, and all fathers are eejits, and worse than eejits. What else would you do with a shovel? Christy was their man. Better yet, the dead man walks onstage. The play has become a horror film, one of those really funny ones. Then Christy gets to fight his Da again, and he wins again. Old Mahon takes his beating and likes it. Christy pushes him offstage, and follows him. 'I'm master of all fights from now.' For the boys in the room, the play ends there. The girls read on, to Pegeen's lament – 'I've lost him surely' – but the boys are offstage with Christy.

The fears of the boys and girls, their dreams, their current selves – they're in *The Playboy*. And – a must for all good school texts – as we read or watch, we see the central characters grow out of their pain, and learn. The first time we see Christy, he's gnawing a turnip. By the end of the play, he's biting Shawn Keogh's leg.

I loved teaching *The Playboy*; it more than made up for *Persuasion*. It's a great school play because it's wild and perfect, much like the average teenager.

When the Moon Has Set

On 23 May 1903 Synge wrote in his diary, 'Finished (?) one act Play When the Moon Has Set (?)'. The question marks betray his own doubts about this early work, but also his determination to express himself as a dramatist. Establishing the pattern he would follow in conscientiously saving all his drafts, this version was labelled 'J'; some time later he returned to the play, producing 'K', also unfinished. Though he marked both 'J' and 'K' 'Rejected', they remained among his papers to be read for possible publication after his death. The following text is based on a collation of these two incomplete but apparently final versions of the play whose ideas he had brooded over since 1896.[2]

The play reflects his deep distress at rejection by his first love Cherrie Matheson because of his refusal to accept

[2] On his second visit to Coole in September 1901 Synge brought with him an earlier complete two-act version. Rejected by Yeats and Lady Gregory, it remained among his papers and was eventually published with a commentary by Mary C. King in *Long Room*, nos.24-25, 1982, the journal of Friends of the Library, Trinity College Dublin. The one-act version published here, a conflation of the final two drafts 'J' and 'K', was first published in J.M.Synge *Plays Book I*, ed. Ann Saddlemyer (Oxford University Press,1968; Colin Smythe, rev. ed. 1982).

Christianity, and his belated attempt to counter her beliefs by rewriting history. But all the drafts also reveal Synge's musical training and the aesthetic, political, and social theories he was developing while studying in Paris, experiencing the realities of life on Aran, and becoming involved in the artistic movements of Dublin. A notebook entry of 1898, repeated in his earlier manuscripts and implicit in this final version reads:

> Every life is a symphony. It is this cosmic element in the person which gives all personal art, and all sincere life, and all passionate love a share in the dignity of the world.

For the first time in this early play, that sequence of notes includes what would become the hallmark of his literary style in the vivid dialogue of the servant Bride and the madwoman Mary Costello, his celebration of the natural world, and his sympathy for those courageous enough to pursue their dreams.

Ann Saddlemyer

When The Moon Has Set

A Play In One Act

Persons

Colm Sweeny, a young man, heir to his uncle's estate
Bride, a young maid
Sister Eileen, a young nun in a nursing order, a distant cousin to Colm
Mary Costello, a madwoman

Scene: A country house in the east of Ireland, late spring or early summer at the turn of the century.

*Old family library in country house; many books are in shelves round the walls. A turf fire has burnt low in the fireplace, which is on one side, with a large portrait above it. The principal door is on the right, but there is another in the back wall partly covered with a curtain and opening with two battants into the open air. Small window near the fireplace; another to the right of the end-door; both have the blinds down. A large lamp heavily shaded is burning near the table. A large bow of black crepe is resting on one of the chairs near the fire. **Bride**, a young maid, is kneeling down settling the turf fire. **Colm** comes in on the left, wearing a big coat buttoned up to his chin.*

Colm: [*looking round the room*]. Sister Eileen has gone to bed?

Bride: She has not, your honour. She's been in a great state fearing you were lost in the hills, and now she's after going down the hollow field to see would there any sound of the wheels coming.

Colm: I came in the other way so she could not have heard me. [*Goes to the large window*] Is she long gone?

Bride: A while only.

Colm: I wonder if I could find her ...

Bride: You could not, your honour, and you'd have a right to be sitting here and warming your feet, the way it's proud and happy she'll be to see you when she turns in from the shower is coming in the trees.

Colm: [*pulling up the blind*]: I hope she will not miss her way. Perhaps if she sees the door open she will turn back. [*He stands looking out.*]

Bride: [*a little impatiently*]. She'll be coming in a minute I'm telling you, and let you be taking your own rest. You're wanting it surely, for we were thinking it's destroyed you'd be driving alone in the night and the great rain, and you not used to anything but the big towns of the world. [*She pulls a chair to the fire.*]

[**Colm** *comes over to the fire, wearily. He begins taking off his coat and heavy boots.* **Bride** *lifts up the bow of crepe from his chair.*]

Bride: [*showing it to him*]. Isn't it a fine bow she's made with bits of rags that we found? I was watching her do it, and I'm telling you she's a wonder surely.

Colm: [*with reserve*]. She is clever with her fingers.

Bride: Wait till your honour sees the way she has the room beyond, with fine flowers in, and white candles, and grand clothes on the bed, and your poor uncle lying so easy with his eyes shut you'd be thinking it was an old man in his sleep. [*Turning to the fire with a sigh.*] Ah, it's a long way any person would go seeking the like of Sister Eileen, and it's very lonesome your honour'll be tomorrow or the next day when she is gone away to the town.

Colm: She will stay for the funeral.

Bride: And what day, if myself may ask, will the funeral be?

Colm: I have settled it for Friday, but it was not easy, there were so many things to arrange.

Bride: It's great trouble the rich do have when there is even an old man to be buried, and it was that, I'm thinking, kept you a whole evening in the town.

Colm: It kept me a good while, but I went wrong going home, and took the road through the bogs to the graveyard of Glan-na-nee.

Bride: The Lord have mercy on us! There does be no one at all passing that way but a few men do be carting turf, and isn't it a great wonder your honour got home safe, and wasn't lost in the hills?

Colm: I hardly knew where I was, but I found a woman there who told me my way.

Bride: It was a lonesome place for a woman, God help her, and the night coming.

Colm: She was nearly crazy I think, but she must have known the trap for she called out to me by my name and asked my uncle.

Bride:[*greatly interested*]. And was it much she said to your honour?

Colm: At first she spoke sensibly and told me how I was to go, but when she tried to say something else she had on her mind she got so confused I could not follow her. Then the mare got frightened at a sort of cry she gave, and I had to come away.

Bride: She was a big tall woman I'm thinking, with a black shawl on her, and black hair round her face? [*She begins blowing the fire with her mouth.*]

Colm: Then you know who she is?

Bride: She's Mary Costello, your honour. [*She goes on blowing.*]

Colm: A beggar woman?

Bride:[*indignantly*]. Not she a beggar woman … She's a Costello from the old Castilian family, and it's fine people they were at one time, big wealthy nobles of the cities of Spain, and herself was the finest girl you'd find in the whole world, with nice manners, and white hands on her, for she was reared with the nuns, as it's likely you've heard tell from his honour, God rest his soul.

Colm: If he ever spoke of her I do not remember it. Why should he have told me about her?

Bride: It's a long story, and a sad pitiful story. I'd have a right to tell you one day maybe if the Lord Almighty keep us alive, but Sister Eileen will be coming now, and the two of you won't be needing the like of that to trouble you at all.

[*She stands up and sweeps up the hearth.*]

Colm: Has she been long out of her mind?

Bride: A long while in and out of it. It's ten years she was below in the Asylum, and it was a great wonder the way you'd see her in there, not lonesome at all with the great lot were coming in from all the houses in the country, and herself as well off as any lady in England, France, or Germany, walking round in the gardens with fine shoes on her feet. Ah, it was well for her in there, God help her, for she was always a nice quiet woman, and a fine woman to look at, and I've heard tell it was 'Your Ladyship' they would call her, the time they'd be making fun among themselves.

Colm: I wonder if I ever saw her before. Her face reminded me of something, or Someone, but I cannot remember where I have met it.

Bride: [*going up to the portrait over the fireplace*]. Let you come and look here, your Honour, and I'm thinking you'll see.

Colm [*going over*]. Yes, that is the woman. But it was done years ago.

Bride: Long years surely, your honour, and it's time the whole thing was forgot, for what call has any man to be weighing his mind with the like of it and he storing sorrows till the judgement day?

[*She goes over to window.* **Colm** *takes down picture and looks at it closely in the lamp-light.*]

Bride: [*looking out*]. Sister Eileen's coming now, and I'll be going off to my bed, for I'm thinking the two of you won't be needing me, and it's a right yourselves would have to be going to rest, and not sitting here talking and talking in the dark night, when people are better sleeping, and not destroying their souls, pausing and watching and they thinking over the great troubles of the world.

[*She goes out, and in a moment* **Sister Eileen** *comes in quickly from the door which leads into the open air. She is pleased and relieved when she sees* **Colm**.]

Sister Eileen: You have come back? I was afraid something had happened.

Colm: I have been in some time.

Sister Eileen: I thought I would hear the wheels, and I went right down to the lake the night is so beautiful …You have arranged everything?

Colm: I sent a number of telegrams, and waited for answers. He is to be buried on Friday at Glan-na-nee, and the coffin will come down tomorrow.

Sister Eileen: When the storm broke I was sorry you had gone; you must have got very wet on the road across the mountains.

Colm: It rained heavily on Slieve na-Ruadh, but I am nearly dry again.

Sister Eileen: I was out for a little while getting flowers for your uncle's room, but I did not find many they were so broken with the rain.

Colm: Then you saw what a change the rain has made among the trees.

Sister Eileen: It has ended the spring. I was just thinking what a difference there is since I arrived here three months ago, with the moonlight shining everywhere on the snow.

Colm: It seems like three years since you telegraphed for me, we have made such a world for ourselves.

Sister Eileen [*changing the subject*]. What have you got there?

Colm: It is the picture from that corner. [*He turns it round to her.*] I saw her tonight at the graveyard of Glan-na-nee.

Sister Eileen: What took you out there, surely that was not your way?

Colm: I went wrong coming home, and this woman put me right. Do you know anything of the woman?

Sister Eileen: I have heard a good deal about her, perhaps more than you have.

Colm: Bride has been telling me that she was a long time in the Asylum, and that she was connected in some way with my uncle.

Sister Eileen: He wanted to marry her although she was beneath him, but when it was all arranged she broke it off because he did not believe in God.

Colm: And after that she went mad?

Sister Eileen: After that. And your uncle shut himself up. He told me it was nearly twenty years since it happened, and yet he had never spoken of it to anyone. I do not think he would have told me if it had not been for his dislike of religious orders and the clothes I wear.

Colm: You mean he told you as a warning … And yet I suppose you take her as an example to be followed.

Sister Eileen: She did what was right. No woman who was really a Christian could have done anything else …

Colm: I wish you had seen her tonight screaming and crying out over the bogs.

Sister Eileen: I do not want to see her … I have seen your uncle for three months and his death today. That is enough.

Colm: It is far from enough if it has not made you realize that in evading her impulses this woman did what was wrong and brought this misery on my uncle and herself.

Sister Eileen [*giving him back the picture*]. We cannot argue about it. We do not see things the same way … Has she changed a great deal since that was done?

Colm: Less than he has. [*He hangs the picture up again.*] He was right in thinking that their story is a warning … At the time they were about the ages we are tonight, and now one is a mad woman, and the other has been tortured to death – [*Some one knocks.*] Come in!

[**Bride**, *half rolled in a shawl, as if she was not fully dressed, comes in with a telegram.*]

Bride: [*giving it to Sister Eileen*]. That has just come for you now,

Sister Eileen: It came into town after Mr. Colm had gone away, and they gave it to an old man was driving out west with an ass and cart.

[**Sister Eileen** *takes it and reads it left.* **Bride** *takes* **Colm** *right.*]

Bride: [*whispering*]. I heard from the old man he seen Mary Costello coming in great haste over the hills, so let your honour not be afeard if you hear her singing or laughing, or letting a shout maybe in the darkness of the night.

Colm: Is there nothing one can do for her?

Bride: Nothing at all your honour. It's best to leave her alone. [*She goes towards the door.*]

Sister Eileen [*turning to her, in a low voice*]. Can someone drive me into the town tomorrow? I must go to Dublin by the first train in the morning.

Bride: We can surely, Sister Eileen. And what time will we send to meet you coming back?

Sister Eileen: I am not coming back.

Bride: Well the Lord speed you Sister Eileen, and that the Almighty God may stretch out a holy hand to preserve and prosper you, and see you safe home. [*Turning to the door.*] It's lonesome you'll be leaving the lot of us behind you, and you after bringing a kind of a new life into this house was a dark quiet place for a score of years, and will be dark again maybe from this mortal night. [*She goes out left.*]

Colm [*with a change in his voice*]. What is this talk of your leaving me tomorrow?

Sister Eileen: Someone has told the Mother Superior your uncle is dead, and she telegraphs – as she puts it – that she is short of nurses and will need me for a new case tomorrow.

Colm: Cannot you stay a little longer?

Sister Eileen: I am afraid not possibly … [*Looking up at the clock.*] I must soon go and pack up.

Colm: We must talk about it till I make you decide with your whole mind whether you will obey the earth, or repeat the story of the mad woman and my uncle.

Sister Eileen [*severely*]. If you say what I think you are wishing to say, I will have to leave you and not speak to you any more. That is all you will gain.

Colm [*sternly, locking door*]. You shall not go till I have said what I have to say. Then if you are weak enough to give up your share of what is best in life, you may go where you will.

Sister Eileen [*piteously*]. I wish you would not spoil the last night we are together.

Colm: It may not be the last ...

Sister Eileen [*goes over and lights candle, picks up bow of crepe*]. Please open the door and let me go to bed. I have been very wrong to allow you to talk to me as I have done, but I will go back to my true life tomorrow, and I will ask to be forgiven.

Colm: And you think you will forget this place and what has been said here?

Sister Eileen: It is only those who do the will of God who are happy; that is all I know.

[*A burst of hysterical laughter is heard outside, and then a sob and a scrap of singing. A moment afterwards the door is pushed open and* **Mary Costello** *comes in, dazzled with the light, and goes over left without seeing* **Colm** *or* **Sister Eileen**. *She goes over to the bureau in the corner and sees that one of the drawers is open and pounces on it. She finds a ring case, and takes out two rings and puts them on her fingers, making the stones sparkle in the lamp light; she finds a bundle of white linen, takes out a silk dress and makes a movement as if she is going to throw it over her head. Before she does so she looks around stealthily, and sees* **Colm** *and* **Sister Eileen**. *She drops the dress on the floor with a cry, picks up her shawl and runs to the door, then stops, and turns towards them.*]

Mary: A nun is it? What right have the like of you to be walking out through the world and looking on us when it isn't any harm we're doing? What right have the nuns I'm saying to be meddling with the world? [*She recognizes* **Colm**.] I seen that man tonight, God bless him, and he driving round on the roads. [*She goes up to him.* **Sister Eileen** *has involuntarily drawn close* *to* **Colm**. **Mary** *looks from one to the other with a peculiar smile.*] You're a fine handsome woman, God bless you, a fine beautiful woman I'm saying, and let you not mind them at all. [*She puts her hand pleadingly on* **Sister Eileen's** *arm.*] Sure you won't mind them, Sister, tell me out you won't mind them at all?

Sister Eileen: Who shall I not mind?

Mary: [*throwing up her hands, and then clasping them together and turning half round with a shriek of laughter*]. 'Who shall I not mind?' says she. 'Who shall I not mind?' It's a long while since I was in school Sister, yet it's well I know the like of that. It's well I know you've no call to mind what the priests say, or the bishops say, or what the angels of God do be saying, for it's little the likes of them knows of women or the seven sorrows of earth. [*With anguish in her voice. She sinks her head and sees the bow of crepe in* **Sister Eileen's** *hand.*] … Who is it is dead, Mister, if that's the token of death?

Colm: My uncle, Colm Sweeny.

Mary: [*indifferently*]. And a long rest behind him, why would that trouble me now? I was afeard it was my little children [*she looks up to* **Colm**, *and speaks piteously*] – for if I was never married your honour, and have no children I do be thinking it's alive they must be if I never had them itself … [*Raising her voice to a plaintive cry.*] I do see them sometimes when my head's bad and I do be falling into my sleep … There are five children, five children that wanted to live, God help them, if the nuns and the priests with them had let me be [*swaying herself with anguish.*] … They're always nice your honour, with clean faces, and nice frocks on them and little sticks in their hands. But I wouldn't like them to begin to die on me, for I'm not like all the rest of [*covering her face with her hands.*] … and it's queer things I do be seeing the time the moon is full. [*She bends her head sobbing piteously.*]

Sister Eileen: Don't mind them now, Mary, there isn't anything to frighten you here.

Mary: [*still sobbing*]. Oh, my head's perished with the night wind, and I do be very lonesome the time I do be going the bog road, with the rabbits running round on it and they drowned with the dew. [*She looks up piteously at* **Sister Eileen,** *sees the little cross she has hanging round her neck; she takes the cross in her hand.*] Will you give me the little cross you have Sister, for I've lost the one I had and I do be wanting the like of it to sit and hold in my hand. [**Sister Eileen** *gives it to her.*] ... May the Almighty God reward you Sister, and give you five nice children before you die. [*She gives her the rings.*] ... May his blessing be on them rings, and they going on your hand, and his blessing be on your hand and it working with the linen when the time is come. [*She looks at the crucifix in her hand.*] ... This will be a quiet thing to be looking on, and it'll keep me still the long evenings when the moon is low, and there do be white mists passing on the bog, the time the little children I have do be lepping, and crying out to each other, and making games in the dark night, and no Christian walking but myself only, and the white geese you'd hear a mile or maybe two mile and they making a great stir over the bog. [*She moves towards the door.*] ... I'll be going now I'm thinking, for I've a long way and this will be keeping me company in the dark lane through the wood. God save you kindly the two of you. There's great marrying in the world but it's late we were surely, and let yourselves not be the same. Let you mind the words I was saying, and give no heed to the priests or the bishops or the angels of God, for it's little the like of them, I was saying, knows about women or the seven sorrows of the earth. [*She goes out.*]

[**Sister Eileen** *goes over and puts the linen and other things back into the drawer.*]

Colm: Another voice has cried out to you. In a few years you will be as old as she is. There will be divine nights like this night and birds crying in the heather, but nothing will reach you, as nothing my uncle at the other side of the hall. [*He goes over to her.*] I am not a woman and I cannot judge of all your feelings, yet I know you have a profound impulse for what is peculiar to women. You realize that the forces which lift women up to a share in the pain and passion of the world are more holy than the vows you have made. [*She stands up before him motionless; he* *speaks more tenderly.*] Before this splendour of the morning you cannot lie. You know that the spirit of life which has transfigured the world is filling you with radiance. Why will you worship the mania of the saints when your own existence is holier than they are. People renounce when they have not power to retain; you have power and courage … I implore you to use them.

Sister Eileen: I don't know what to do … You are giving me such pain and yet …

Colm: There is the first note of the birds … When the sun comes over that ridge I will ask you to be my wife … You cannot refuse. The trees might as well refuse to grow fragrant and green when it is May, or the birds to sing before the dawn … There are the larks, and the wrens … You have half an hour. I will not touch you … I will not try to persuade you. It is quite unnecessary. The world will persuade you. The breath that drew out this forest of leaves and sent quivering voices to chant in them, is making of you also a beautiful note in the world … There is the willow warbler, you have a quarter of an hour. Will you go and put this dress about you. I am not in a humour for blasphemy.

[**Sister Eileen** *takes the green dress and goes out without looking at him. He looks out for an instant, then packs the rest of the papers into the bureau drawer. He goes back to the window. In a moment* **Sister Eileen** *comes in behind him in a green silk dress which is cut low at the neck. She reaches the window just as the red morning light sweeps into the room.*]

Sister Eileen [*in a low voice*]. Colm, I have come back to you.

Colm [*turning towards her*]. You are infinitely beautiful, and you have done a great action. It is the beauty of your spirit that has set you free, and your emancipation is more exquisite than any that is possible for men who are redeemed by logic. You cannot tell me why you have changed. That is your glory. As a moth comes out to a new sphere of odour and colour and flight, so you have come out to live in a new sphere of beautiful love … Listen to the tumult the birds are making in the trees. That is